Acknowledgements

Lexomics research has been supported for many years by the generosity of Wheaton College, the Teagle Foundation, the Mars, Hood and Clemence families, the Mellon Foundation, Central Children's Charities, and the National Endowment for the Humanities, who sponsored the research in three grants: NEH HD-50300-08, "Pattern Recognition through Computational Stylistics: Old English and Beyond" 2008–2009; NEH PR-50112011, "Lexomic Tools and Methods for Textual Analysis: Providing Deep Access to Digitized Texts" 2011–2013; and NEH HD-228732-15, National Endowment for the Humanities, Digital Humanities Start-up grant: "Easing Entry and Improving Access to Computer-Assisted Text Analysis for the Humanities," 2015–2017. Any views, findings, conclusions, or recommendations expressed in this article do not necessarily reflect those of the National Endowment for the Humanities.

This research would not have been possible without the efforts of Michael J. Kahn and Mark D. LeBlanc. The authors would also like to thank Scott Kleinman, Sarah Downey, Leonard Neidorf, Carol Mannix, Veronica Kerekes, Rosetta M. Berger, Elie Chauvet, Rachel Scavera, Namiko Hitotsubashi, Courtney LaBrie, Ann Marie Brasacchio, Yun Meng, Jillian Valerio, Rowan Lowell, Cora Kohn, Audrey Dubois, Chloë Urbanczyk, Elizabeth Crowley, John Segal, Jonathan Gerkin, Elizabeth Peterson and Sarah Creese. The software that enabled this research was developed by multiple teams of developers. Thanks to Christina Nelson, Amos Jones, Donald Bass, Richard Neal, Alicia Herbert, Douglas Raffle, Bryan Jensen, Julia Morneau, Devin Delfino, Vicky Li, Qi Zhang, Lithia Helmreich, Jinnan Ge, Sarah Zhang, Cheng Zhang, Shiwei Huang, Austin Gillis, Caleb Wastler, Jesse Aronson and Jianxiang Lui.

Beowulf Unlocked

Michael D.C. Drout • Yvette Kisor •
Leah Smith • Allison Dennett • Natasha Piirainen

Beowulf Unlocked

New Evidence from Lexomic Analysis

Michael D.C. Drout
Wheaton College
Dedham, Massachusetts, USA

Yvette Kisor
Ramapo College of New Jersey
Mahwah, New Jersey, USA

Leah Smith
Artist and Independent Scholar
Providence, Rhode Island, USA

Allison Dennett
Independent Scholar
Portsmouth, New Hampshire, USA

Natasha Piirainen
Independent Scholar
Mechanic Falls, Maine, USA

ISBN 978-3-319-30627-8   ISBN 978-3-319-30628-5 (eBook)
DOI 10.1007/978-3-319-30628-5

Library of Congress Control Number: 2016943528

© The Editor(s) (if applicable) and The Author(s) 2016
This work is subject to copyright. All rights are solely and exclusively licensed by the Publisher, whether the whole or part of the material is concerned, specifically the rights of translation, reprinting, reuse of illustrations, recitation, broadcasting, reproduction on microfilms or in any other physical way, and transmission or information storage and retrieval, electronic adaptation, computer software, or by similar or dissimilar methodology now known or hereafter developed.
The use of general descriptive names, registered names, trademarks, service marks, etc. in this publication does not imply, even in the absence of a specific statement, that such names are exempt from the relevant protective laws and regulations and therefore free for general use.
The publisher, the authors and the editors are safe to assume that the advice and information in this book are believed to be true and accurate at the date of publication. Neither the publisher nor the authors or the editors give a warranty, express or implied, with respect to the material contained herein or for any errors or omissions that may have been made.

Printed on acid-free paper

This Palgrave Macmillan imprint is published by Springer Nature
The registered company is Springer International Publishing AG Switzerland

Contents

1	Introduction	1
2	Lexomic Methods	5
3	Text Preparation of *Beowulf*	17
4	Cluster Analysis of *Beowulf*	23
5	Interpretation of the Cluster Analysis	55
6	Conclusions Drawn from Cluster Analysis	81
Bibliography		85
Index		91

LIST OF FIGURES

Fig. 2.1	Sample dendrogram	9
Fig. 2.2	Ribbon diagram of a hypothetical text with five internal divisions (1–5) separated into six segments (A–F)	11
Fig. 2.3	Illustration of blending	13
Fig. 4.1	Ribbon diagram of *Beowulf*	25
Fig. 4.2	Dendrogram of *Beowulf* KL4 divided into 1200-word segments	26
Fig. 4.3	KL4 segmented at 1200, segments C1 and B1 hinted to isolate the Unferth/Breca episode in C1	29
Fig. 4.4	KL4 hinted and blended A-Scribe material	32
Fig. 4.5	A-Scribe scrabble diagram	34
Fig. 4.6	Screening dendrogram of lines 1939–3182 of KL4 in 900-word segments	37
Fig. 4.7	KL4 B-Scribe text after hinting, segment J excluded	41
Fig. 4.8	B-Scribe scrabble diagram	42
Fig. 4.9	Normalized KL4 in 1200-word segments	43
Fig. 4.10	Normalized KL4 after hinting and blending	44
Fig. 4.11	Normalized KL4 after hinting and blending, segments K and P merged	45
Fig. 4.12	Normalized KL4 after hinting and blending, segments M, N1 and O1 merged	46
Fig. 4.13	Full poem scrabble diagram	51

LIST OF TABLES

Table 2.1	Calculation of relative frequency of *æfter* in three segments of a hypothetical text	7
Table 2.2	Calculation of distances (in terms of the distribution of *æfter*) in three segments of a hypothetical text	8
Table 4.1	Line numbers for 1200-word segments of *Beowulf*	24
Table 4.2	Segment boundaries in Fig. 4.4, KL4 A-Scribe, material hinted and blended	33

CHAPTER 1

Introduction

Abstract New methods of "lexomic" analysis can shed light on even a poem as well-studied as *Beowulf*.

Keywords Lexomics • Lexomic methods • *Beowulf* • Digital humanities

In a field as mature as *Beowulf* studies, the discovery of new data is a rare event. Possessed of a two-hundred-year critical history written by generations of sharp-eyed scholars, the text of *Beowulf* would seem to have yielded all extractable information, and indeed, the larger recent debates in the field have been over the interpretation of the evidence already accumulated. The possibility of discovering *new* evidence has not been much entertained, and reasonably so: the chance that a trove of Anglo-Saxon manuscripts relating to *Beowulf* could come to light is infinitesimal, and even the most remarkable archeological discoveries[1] are unlikely to be directly applicable to the text of the poem itself. Furthermore, in the past three decades philological and linguistic methods, previously so productive, have failed to uncover many new facts,[2] suggesting, perhaps, that their capabilities are exhausted or that *Beowulf* is simply mined out. But just as advances in technology allow valuable minerals to be recovered from abandoned tailings heaps, innovations in information processing may enable us to extract new data from old texts: in both cases the technology allows us concentrate that which was previously too diffuse to be useful.

© The Editor(s) (if applicable) and The Author(s) 2016
M.D.C. Drout et al., *Beowulf Unlocked*,
DOI 10.1007/978-3-319-30628-5_1

In this study we present the results of our use of "lexomic"[3] methods to analyze the text of *Beowulf*. These approaches, which use computer-assisted statistical analyses to augment traditional philological and literary techniques, have identified patterns of vocabulary distribution, meter and orthography that, when examined in light of our previous knowledge of the poem, shed new light on *Beowulf*'s structure, ontogeny and evolution. In this first half of a two-part investigation, we introduce methods of *cluster analysis* that allow us to calculate and represent visually the relative similarity of the vocabulary distributions of segments of a text. Previous research has shown that, in other Anglo-Saxon texts, these patterns of vocabulary distribution are often correlated with sources, structures and histories. Here, we show how the methods can be adapted to the particular problems posed by *Beowulf* and that, when combined with more traditional approaches to the poem, cluster analyses can identify relationships of similarity and difference between various sections of *Beowulf* that might otherwise be too subtle or diffuse to be detected by the unaided eye and mind.[4]

Since the earliest days of *Beowulf* scholarship researchers have sought to use the poem in support of arguments about other questions (some only tangentially related to *Beowulf* itself).[5] This tendentious approach has regularly led to significant data being misconstrued or misunderstood and to the insights of previous scholars being neglected.[6] Even in more recent studies, in which *Beowulf* is not used for explicitly nationalistic or other overtly partisan political purposes, observation has often been subordinated to thesis, with the predictable result that some data are under- and others over-emphasized, making it difficult for a logical synthesis to evolve. We seek to avoid this problem—at least as long as possible—by describing the tools and methods and then presenting the data acquired by them without trying to embed interpretive or synthetic conclusions in the discussion (these we will leave for the final sections of each part of the investigation).[7] The goal of this structure is to allow interested researchers to adopt those methodologies that they find congenial without by so doing being manipulated, rhetorically or logically, into pre-accepting a specific position on later interpretations.[8] To avoid having each piece of new evidence become, at the very moment of its production, entangled in the thicket of the major scholarly disputes, parts of this paper operate at a higher level of abstraction than has been traditional in *Beowulf* studies. We also, for the most part, reserve until the interpretative section of the paper references to the rich scholarship to be found on nearly every line of the poem. Readers should not infer from this arrangement any rejection of the painstaking, erudite analysis of the details of the poem, the accumulation of which is an intellectual monument. We are merely trying to make our own argument as clear, unencumbered and straightforward as possible, emphasizing the findings and the methods that have produced them.

Notes

1. The National Endowment for the Humanities helped sponsor this research with three grants: NEH HD-50300-08, "Pattern Recognition through Computational Stylistics: Old English and Beyond" 2008-2009; NEH PR-50112011, "Lexomic Tools and Methods for Textual Analysis: Providing Deep Access to Digitized Texts" 2011-13; and NEH HD-228732-15. National Endowment for the Humanities, Digital Humanities Start-up grant: "Easing Entry and Improving Access to Computer-Assisted Text Analysis for the Humanities," 2015-17. Any views, findings, conclusions, or recommendations expressed in this article do not necessarily reflect those of the National Endowment for the Humanities.
2. In great part due to their being perfected over multiple scholarly generations.
3. Derived by analogy from "genomics," the term "lexomics" was coined by Betsey Dexter Dyer in 2002 and first appeared in print in *Genome Technology* 1.27 (2002).
4. Clustering methods do have a weakness in that they, by necessity, require us to compare reasonably large segments of a text, limiting the sizes of features that we can resolve. Additionally, cluster methods detect relationships that are discrete rather than continuous, thus making the detection and selection of ideal segment boundaries a matter of trial and error. We overcome some of these limitations in the follow-up to this study, Beowulf Unlocked II: The Evidence of Rolling Window Analysis [forthcoming], in which we use *rolling window analysis* to allow us to resolve features that are both continuous and smaller than those identified by cluster analysis. Rolling window analysis enables us to depict the distribution of metrical, linguistic and orthographic features more accurately, identifying concentrations and allowing us to correlate them with the results of both cluster analysis and more traditional approaches. Combined, the two lexomic techniques compensate for each other's deficiencies and significantly enhance the knowledge already gained from traditional approaches.
5. See, among others, Allen J. Frantzen, *Desire for Origins: New Language, Old English and Teaching the Tradition*. New Brunswick: Rutgers University Press, 1990, 168–200; T. A. Shippey and Andreas Haarder, *Beowulf: The Critical Heritage*. London: Routledge 1998, 1–74 and *passim*; T. A. Shippey, *The Shadow-Walkers: Jacob Grimm's Mythology of the Monstrous*. Tempe: Arizona

Center for Medieval and Renaissance Texts and Studies, 2005; Joep Leerssen, *National Thought in Europe: A Cultural History*. Amsterdam: Amsterdam University Press, 2006; Andrew Wawn, Graham Johnson and John Walter, *Constructing Nations, Reconstructing Myth: Essay in Honour of T. A. Shippey*. Turnhout: Brepols, 2007.

6. Theodore Andersson's assessment that "the institutional memory in *Beowulf* studies is about an even century" may even be optimistic. Theodore Andersson, "Sources and Analogues," in Robert E. Bjork and John D. Niles, eds. *A Beowulf Handbook*. Lincoln, NE: University of Nebraska Press, 1998, 129.

7. In so doing we will try to live up to the example of Levin Schücking, who in 1905 showed that it was possible to present evidence both for and against a preferred argument and to be fair-minded when evaluating it and the arguments of others. Levin Schücking, *Beowulfs Rückkehr: eine kritische Studie*. Studien zur englischen Philologie 21. Halle: Max Niemeyer, 1905.

8. We are trying to avoid presenting our argument as a "case lawyer's plea," instead seeking to set out the evidence "in clear detail for a sober and dispassionate judge"; Johan Gerritsen, "Have with you to Lexington! The *Beowulf* Manuscript and *Beowulf*," in *In Other Words, Transcultural Studies in Philology, Translation and Lexicography Presented to Hans Heinrich Meier on the Occasion of his Sixty-Fifth Birthday*, ed. J. Mackenzie and R. Todd, Dordrecht: Foris, 1989, 15–34 at 15.

CHAPTER 2

Lexomic Methods

Abstract New "lexomic" methods combine computer-assisted statistical analysis with traditional philological, source-study and close-reading literary approaches. Hierarchical agglomerative cluster analysis is used to identify segments of a poem that have distinctively different (or similar) vocabulary distributions, and traditional methods are then employed to explain why the segments are very similar to or different from each other. A variety of techniques are used to identify the boundaries of segments, including "hinting" and "blending." Dendrogram geometries are interpreted in light of previous research in Old English and other cultural and literary traditions.

Keywords Lexomics • Lexomic methods • *Beowulf* • Dendrogram • Hierarchical agglomerative cluster analysis • Segmentation • Hinting • Blending

The term "lexomics" refers to an evolving set of methods of textual analysis that combine computer-assisted statistical analysis with traditional literary scholarship, using the results of each to explain those of the other. The methods have some of their immediate sources in the young discipline of bioinformatics, and they also draw on the computational stylometrics pioneered by scholars like John Burrows[1] and David Hoover.[2] In contrast to corpus linguistics and some computational stylometry (and also contra Franco Moretti's call for "distant reading"[3]), lexomic methods include a regular use of traditional close reading, philological analysis, source study and interpretation. The traditional approaches come both first and last in a repeatable three-part sequence: we first read and interpret in order to find areas in which lexomic approaches may be useful or questions that they might answer; we then employ the computer-assisted statistical methods as a "middle game"[4] that helps us test hypotheses and discover new relationships; and finally, we use close reading and interpretation to understand the results of our analyses. This sequence can be iterated as many times as necessary, with adjustments made at all three stages.

Although, as we shall see, *Beowulf* presents some significant challenges, we can, based on previous research, be reasonably confident of the utility of lexomic approaches. The methods have both led to conclusions consistent with traditional forms of analysis and shed new light on a variety of texts in multiple traditions. In examples of the former, lexomic methods were able to identify lines 235–851 of *Genesis* as having a different source than the rest of that poem, a conclusion consistent with Sievers' deduction from a century and a half ago but using completely different forms of analysis.[5] The methods also correctly identified the parallel (but not *verbatim*) lines of *Azarias* and *Daniel* and further supported the conclusion that portions of *Daniel* are influenced by Latin canticles[6] (and a lost Old English text)[7] rather than being based directly upon the Latin biblical text that is the source for the rest of the poem. Lexomic analysis also accurately identified the divisions of the three *Christ* and two *Guthlac* poems of the Exeter Book and correctly clustered together the poems of Cynewulf.[8] The methods were able to distinguish between the sections of the Old English translation of Orosius's *Historiae adversus paganos* that are translated directly from the primary source and those that were not, and to differentiate between the sections of the Old English Penitential based on an Anglo-Saxon source and those translated from Latin.[9] Lexomic approaches have also improved our understanding of the textual history of *Guthlac A*,[10] supported the Cynewulfian affiliation of *Guthlac B*,[11] and provided evidence that an Old English text of the *Song of the Three Youths* pre-dated *Daniel*.[12] Lexomic analysis has also been successfully applied to texts in medieval Latin,[13] Old Norse,[14] Middle English, and modern English.[15] There are thus many good reasons to think that lexomic methods can be used successfully to investigate *Beowulf*.[16]

2.1 Hierarchical Agglomerative Cluster Analysis

Hierarchical cluster analysis uses the mathematical calculation of similarity and distance to group entities in such a way that those within a group or cluster share more features than those outside the group. When used to investigate texts, cluster analysis compares the distribution of words to produce visual representations of the relative similarities and differences of the texts being examined. Our approach builds upon previous work in computer-assisted stylometry, but it differs in three important ways. First, almost all previous researchers used only subsets of the words in a text (for example, only content- or function-words), while we include every word in our analyses. Second, we adopt a "bag of words" approach that relies only on vocabulary distribution and thus allows us to avoid the labor-intensive (and subjective) problems of encoding syntactic or semantic information. Third and most distinctively, instead of focusing on similarities among or differences between whole texts, we divide texts into segments and analyze the relationships of these to each other. This segmentation appears to enable more accurate analysis than undivided-text comparisons and allows us to detect the influence of sources or multiple authors[17] and to identify textual features at a higher resolution.

After a text has been prepared for analysis (discussed below in § 3) we divide it into segments and then tabulate the words in both the entire text and in each segment. We then calculate the relative frequency of each word in each segment by dividing the number of times the word appears by the total number of words in that segment.[18] For example, if a text is divided into two 1000-word and one 985-word segments and the word *æfter* appears ten times in segment 1, seven times in segment 2, and five times in segment 3, we can produce a table of relative frequencies like that in Table 2.1.

We then calculate the difference between the relative frequencies of each word in each segment, square each word's distance, and take the

Table 2.1 Calculation of relative frequency of *æfter* in three segments of a hypothetical text

	Segment 1	*Segment 2*	*Segment 3*
Segment size	1000	1000	985
Appearances of *æfter*	10	7	5
Relative frequency of *æfter*	0.010	0.007	0.005

square-root of the sum of these squared differences to find the Euclidian distance[19] between each pair of segments. We then use the free implementation of hierarchical, agglomerative clustering to group segments, without pre-specifying the number of groups into which they will be arranged, by finding those segments that have the shortest distances between them. For example, if we list the difference in relative frequencies of *after* for each pair of segments in our hypothetical three-segment text, we can see that the difference between segment 2 and segment 3 is the smallest. These segments, therefore, form the first pair in a cluster. The distances between the remaining segments and the midpoint of a line connecting segments 2 and 3 are now compared and the closest segment is joined to the first pair. The process continues until all segments have been added. Because distance is scalar, it can be calculated for the entire n-dimensional array of words and therefore used to determine the similarities of texts that contain many different words (Table 2.2).

From these groupings and their distances from each other, we produce a branching diagram, or *dendrogram*, that visually represents the relative similarities of the segments. Figure 2.1 illustrates the similarities of four hypothetical segments. Dissimilarity between clades is represented by the length of the vertical line connecting them.[20] Sub-levels of the dendrogram are called *clades*, which we label from left to right using Greek letters, first marking all clades at the same level of the hierarchy and then descending to the next level and again labeling left to right. Thus in Fig. 2.1, clade α contains segment A, clade β contains B, C, and D, and clade γ contains only segments C and D. A clade with no subsidiary branches, like clade α, is said to be *simplicifolious*, or single-leafed.[21]

Table 2.2 Calculation of distances (in terms of the distribution of *after*) in three segments of a hypothetical text

Segment pair	Distance
Segment 1 to Segment 2	0.003
Segment 2 to Segment 3	0.002
Segment 1 to Segment 3	0.005

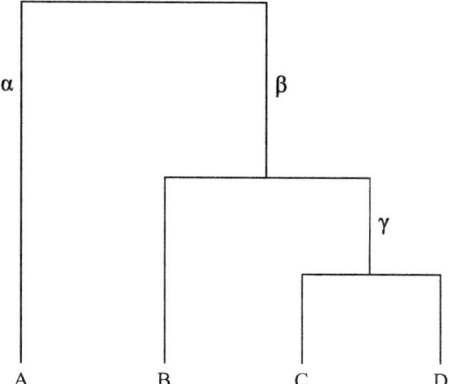

Fig. 2.1 Sample dendrogram

A dendrogram represents dissimilarity between segments by the vertical length of the line between branch-points: the shorter the line, the more similar the clades. The geometry of the dendrogram in Fig. 2.1 indicates that segments C and D are most similar, segment B is closer to clade γ, which contains both C and D, and segment A is least like the other texts. Dendrograms can be read from the top down, identifying higher-level patterns of similarity and difference, or from the bottom up, identifying individual segments that are most similar to each other.

2.2 Interpreting Dendrogram Geometries

Dendrogram geometries, which represent distributions of vocabulary, are often correlated with other features of a text, including sources and structure. Leaves or clades that are significantly separated from the main body of a dendrogram often contain material drawn from sources different from those of the main text. For example, in a dendrogram of the Old English *Genesis*, the lines of the poem than have an Old Saxon source (235–851) appear in a different clade than those that were translated from

Latin.[22] Similarly, a dendrogram of *Guthlac A* indicates that a segment containing lines 499–676, the famous hellmouth scene, has a proximate source different from that of the rest of that poem.[23] In Old English prose, those sections of the Anglo-Saxon translation of Orosius' *Historiae adversus paganos* based on non-Orosian geographical materials, as well as the accounts of the voyages of Ohthere and Wulfstan, cluster separately from the main text.[24]

As well as indicating differences of sourcing, textual history or structure, dendrogram geometry can also reflect affinities among segments of multiple texts. For example, the poem *Azarias* clusters with the segment of *Daniel* to which it is parallel even though the similarity is not word-for-word. The final two segments of *Guthlac B*, long suspected to be by the poet Cynewulf, cluster with the signed poems of that poet.[25] The sections of the *Old English Penitential* that are based on Latin sources cluster together and are separate from those whose source is the Old English *Scriftboc*.[26]

Not only can individual dendrogram geometries be explained by the sources and structure of a text, but some general shapes are typical of certain underlying characteristics of a text. Most significantly, a *stepwise* dendrogram, which begins with a single pair of segments to which each subsequent segment adds individually (i.e., a structure with little hypotaxis) and which is characterized by short vertical distances between the branch points is diagnostic of a text with a homogeneous vocabulary distribution.[27]

Through trial and error and by comparison with control texts whose sourcing or structure has previously been determined by traditional approaches, we have learned that clustering methods are reasonably accurate with segment-sizes as small as 500 and as large as 2000 words. Segments smaller than 500 words at times produce statistical artifacts; larger segments can obscure the relationships of similarity we are trying to detect[28] but as long as we keep segments generally within this range and do not make them differ massively in size from each other, we can be reasonably confident that segment size alone is not skewing the results of the analysis.

More challenging than setting segment size is the problem of determining the boundaries of segments in texts whose sources or structures are unknown, ambiguous or disputed. Because hierarchical agglomerative cluster analysis uses simple distance metrics, the mixing together of the features of multiple sub-units can, when segment boundaries do not end up coinciding with sources or structural aspects of the text, produce *artifacts*, false similarities or differences that are not representative of the underlying text. For example, in the *ribbon diagram* in Fig. 2.2, we see that sub-units 1, 3 and 5 are similar to each other and different from the pair of 2 and 4. But if the text is divided in such a way as to produce segments A–F, we will get a dendrogram with segment A and F linked together and separately from the grouping of B, C, D, and E. The metaphor of color is perhaps helpful as an intuition pump: sub-units 1, 3, and 5 are red, while 2 and 4 are blue. But because the similarities of entire segments are calculated in the distance metric, a given sectioning of the text could produce two red (A and F) and three purple segments (B, C, D, E).[29] The apparent similarity among the purple segments is artifactual, as it does not reflect the actual similarities of the sub-units. Thus we see that if the segment-boundaries do not isolate distinct sub-sections, a heterogeneous text can produce false homogeneity.

There are several ways to identify distinct segment boundaries even in texts whose underlying sources or structures are not known. In all of them, we produce multiple dendrograms in which we have varied both segment sizes and boundaries. We then correlate these dendrograms with a ribbon diagram of the text to determine which sections of the text most consistently cluster together despite variations in segment sizes or boundaries.

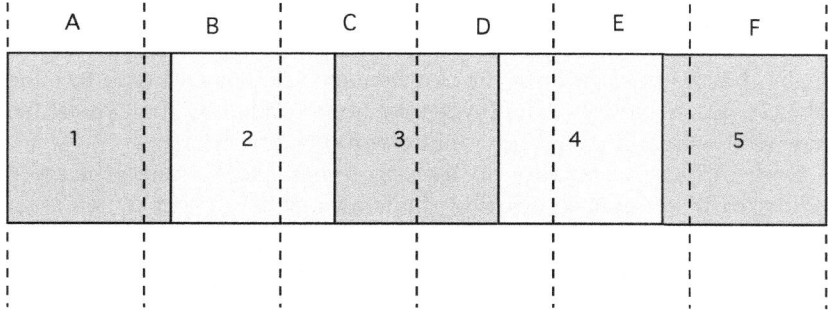

Fig. 2.2 Ribbon diagram of a hypothetical text with five internal divisions (1–5) separated into six segments (A–F)

For example, in the text represented in Fig. 2.2, we could experiment with large segments made up of all of A and half of B (a1), the second half of B and all of C (b1), the second half of C and all of D (c1), and a short segment made up of only the second half of E (d1). If b1 and c1 still clustered together, we would be able to conclude that the material that made B similar to the other segments was concentrated in the second half of B. Sub-sections of the text that consistently group together are identifies as having *robust* relationships, which are likely to indicate the underlying sources or structure of the text.

However, there are cases in which a single segment size cannot produce boundaries that do not artificially divide or conflate possible structures or sources of the poem. Segments of 1000 words, for instance, must fall along plausible boundaries for the majority of a text but cut through one particular speech or description. For unevenly structured texts it is often not possible, even using the techniques discussed above, to devise a consistent interval that does not divide natural or apparent sub-sections of the text. In these cases, we take advantage of our calculations being based on relative frequency rather than absolute count by *hinting* the segment boundaries until they match up with the nearest reasonable syntactic or narrative divisions. For example, in the text depicted in Fig. 2.2, we could shift the boundary of segment c1 to eliminate the short segment d1 and make that material part of the larger, preceding segment.

Blending, a more labor-intensive technique, is useful in situations where we think that short sub-sections of a text might be interwoven too closely to isolate them using only shifting and hinting. To blend, we divide adjacent segments and match the first half of the first segment with the first half of the second. Thus in Fig. 2.3 we divide segments A and B into a1, a2, b1, b2 and then produce the new blended segments A1 (a1 + b1) and B1 (a2 + b2). We use blending when we hope to identify similarities that may be obscured by a structure of interwoven short segments.

Both of these techniques do have the potential to create artifacts as well as to reveal actually existing similarities. When a text is heterogeneous in vocabulary distribution, the inter-relationships of text segments can behave as a dynamical system in which small shifts of boundaries can result in large-scale changes to the geometry of the entire dendrogram. To cope with such problems, we vary segment sizes and boundaries, producing many dendrograms with slightly different parameters and identifying robust patterns in the resultant geometries. Even if the overall structure of a dendrogram shifts when small adjustments are made to segment

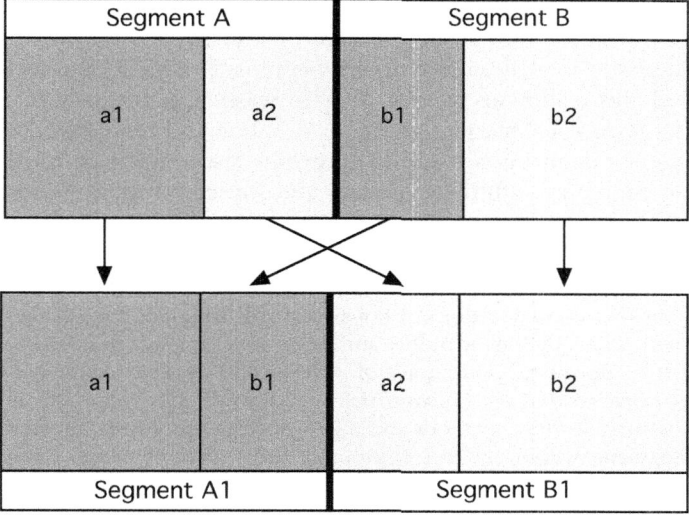

Fig. 2.3 Illustration of blending

boundaries, if material from two particular sub-sections is consistently grouped together, that grouping is robust and thus potentially of interest.

Three additional techniques help us to identify robust clades. In *shifting* we begin with a division at fixed intervals and then shift all boundaries by a regular number of words in order to see how small changes affect the geometries of the resulting dendrograms. In *truncation*, we produce a dendrogram of the entire text and then delete segments one by one, observing any abrupt changes in overall geometry when a particular segment is removed. *Incrementation* is simply reverse truncation, in which we begin with two segments and add other segments to them one at a time, observing the way the dendrogram evolves. Both truncation and incrementation allow us to identify keystone relationships among segments: when the presence or absence of half of a particular pairing radically reshapes a dendrogram we know that the pairing is robust.

By using these techniques to compare multiple dendrograms, we can improve the resolution of our analysis, allowing us to identify features of interest that are somewhat smaller than the 500–750-word-length windows that limit dendrogram analysis. More detailed resolution can in some cases be accomplished via the methods of rolling window analysis (discussed in the follow-up monograph to this study), but for our present purposes it is sufficient to note in summary that: (1) the techniques described above allow us to identify with reasonable accuracy the degree of similarity of vocabulary in segments of a text and represent these relationships in a dendrogram; and (2) previous research has correlated dendrogram geometry with the structures and sources of Anglo-Saxon texts.

Notes

1. Burrows uses collections of function words to build textual "signatures," with which he then identifies authors in some English Restoration poems. J. F. Burrows, "Questions of Authorship: Attribution and Beyond," *Computers and the Humanities* 37 (2003): 5–32. There are similarities between lexomic methods and Burrows' delta procedure, but we compare segments within one text or group of texts, while he takes a corpus-based approach. The delta procedure compares texts by the mean differences for each word from a representative set of works from the text's era and genre. See John F. Burrows, "The Englishing of Juvenal: Computational Stylistics and Translated Texts," *Style* 36, no. 4 (2002): 677.
2. Hoover has further refined Burrows' methods and applied them to prose in third-person American novels. David L. Hoover, "Testing Burrows's Delta," *Literary and Linguistic Computing* 19, no. 4 (2004): 453–475.
3. Franco Moretti, *Graphs, Maps and Trees: Abstract Models for a Literary History*. London: Verso 2005, 4–5.
4. Burrows' term.
5. Michael D. C. Drout, Michael J. Kahn, Mark D. LeBlanc and Christina Nelson, "Of Dendrogrammatology: Lexomic Methods for Analyzing the Relationships Among Old English Poems," *Journal of English and Germanic Philology* 110 (2011): 301–336.
6. Drout et al., "Of Dendrogrammatology," 307–311, 326–328.
7. Michael D. C. Drout and Elie Chauvet, "Tracking the Moving Ratio of þ to ð in Anglo-Saxon Texts: A New Method, and Evidence for a lost Old English version of the 'Song of the Three Youths,'" *Anglia* 133, no. 2 (2015): 278–319.
8. Drout et al., "Of Dendrogrammatology," 319–326, 333–335.
9. Phoebe Boyd, Michael D. C. Drout, Namiko Hitotsubashi, Michael J. Kahn, Mark D. LeBlanc and Leah Smith. "Lexomic Analysis of Anglo-Saxon Prose: Establishing Controls with the Old English Penitential and the Old English translation of Orosius." *Revista de la Sociedad Española de Lengua y Literatura Inglesa Medieval (SELIM)* 19 (2014): 7–58 at 25–35.

10. Sarah Downey, Michael D. C. Drout, Michael J. Kahn and Mark D. LeBlanc, "'Books Tell Us': Lexomic and Traditional Evidence for the Sources of *Guthlac A*," *Modern Philology* 110 (2012): 1–29.
11. Drout et al., "Of Dendrogrammatology," 323–326.
12. Drout and Chauvet, 19–27.
13. Sarah Downey, Michael D. C. Drout, Veronica Kerekes and Douglas Raffle, "Lexomic Analysis of Medieval Latin Texts," *Journal of Medieval Latin* 24 (2014): 225–274.
14. Rosetta Berger and Michael D. C. Drout, "A Reconsideration of the Relationship Between *Víga-Glúms Saga* and *Reykdæla Saga*: New Evidence from Lexomic Analysis," *Viking and Medieval Scandinavia* 11 (2015): 1–32.
15. Michael D. C. Drout, Namiko Hitotsubashi and Rachel Scavera, "Tolkien's Creation of the Impression of Depth." *Tolkien Studies* 11 (2014): 167–211; Michael D. C. Drout, Elizabeth Peterson, Ann Marie Brasacchio and Yun Meng, "Lexomic Analysis of Shakespeare's Collaborations," [forthcoming].
16. The first question we are asked at most presentations about the lexomic analysis of Anglo-Saxon literature is invariably "What about *Beowulf*?"
17. Although the information we recover with our methods may have some bearing on questions of authorship, our analyses have not to this point focused primarily on author identification but instead on a text's sources or affinities; Drout et al., "Of Dendrogrammatology," 323–326.
18. Although for the sake of convenience we often use round-number segment divisions, the use of relative frequencies allows us to compare segments of varying sizes. For example, if there are 935 words in a segment and *æfter* appears 12 times, we record $12/935 = .0128$ as the relative frequency. If a word appears somewhere in the complete text but not in a particular segment, we record $0/n = 0$ for the word's relative frequency in that segment.
19. This metric makes use of all n words in a collection of texts to measure the dissimilarity between two texts. We also experimented with Manhattan and Canberra metrics but found no significant difference in the final clustering results. The Lexos software allows researchers to choose among these metrics and between different linkage methods.
20. In our lexomic analyses the number of words is quite large, so it is difficult for the distributions of any single word to make two segments highly similar or dissimilar. A great deal of commonality (or difference) in the proportionate use of a wide array of words is required to create significant similarity (or distance) between two texts. See the discussion in Drout et al., "Of Dendrogrammatology," 311–315.
21. The term *haplophyllic* is sometimes used instead of *simplicifolious*.

22. Drout et al., "Of Dendrogrammatology," 315–319.
23. Downey et al., "Books Tell Us," 176–181.
24. Boyd et al., 35–46.
25. Drout et al., "Of Dendrogrammatology," 323–325.
26. Boyd et al., 25–35.
27. Drout et al., "Of Dendrogrammatology," 311–315.
28. Drout et al., "Of Dendrogrammatology," 311–315.
29. For example, when the portion of the Old English poem *Christ III* that is based on a sermon of Caesarius of Arles is divided in such a way that one segment is 10% sermon, 90% normal text, while the next segment is 50% sermon, 50% normal text, the 10% segment may not cluster with the 50% segment but instead with segments that are 100% normal text. See Drout et al., "Of Dendrogrammatology," 320–323; Downey et al., "Books Tell Us," 168–171.

CHAPTER 3

Text Preparation of *Beowulf*

Abstract The chapter discusses the particular problems that *Beowulf* poses for lexomic analysis, among them the differing orthography of the two scribes and wide variation among scholarly editions of the poem. The decision to use the fourth edition of Fr. Klaeber's *Beowulf* as a base text is explained, as are the various techniques used for processing the text. Procedures for creating a self-normalized text of *Beowulf* are also detailed.

Keywords *Beowulf* • Electronic editions • Processing • Normalization • Diplomatic vs. critical editions

In order to perform cluster analysis and produce dendrograms, we must remove from electronic texts those features that are not relevant to the comparison of vocabulary or which could generate false positives or negatives. This process, which we call *scrubbing*, eliminates formatting, punctuation and numerals and makes all capital letters lower-case. We also remove tagging and other mark-ups, such as the labeling of corrections or foreign words.[1]

3.1 Text Preparation: Orthography

The special characters found in Old English texts, most significantly *thorn* <þ>, *eth* <ð> and Tironian note, 7, present a particular set of problems.[2] The phonetic equivalence of *thorn* and *eth* can introduce false negatives into an analysis if, for example, *þis* and *ðis* are counted as two different words. To eliminate this problem, we can replace all *eths* with *thorns* (a process we call *consolidation*). However, there are times when the distinction between *þis* and *ðis* might be relevant to an analysis, in which case consolidation would eliminate potentially useful data. We have experimented with both consolidated and unconsolidated texts and have found that, in general, consolidation only changes dendrogram geometry when multiple segments of a text are characterized by patterns of orthography whose differences are consistent, a relatively rare occurrence within most Anglo-Saxon poems.[3] Unfortunately for the present analysis, *Beowulf* is one case in which consolidated and unconsolidated texts produce dendrograms with significantly differing geometries and so, as discussed below, simple consolidation was not sufficient.

Tironian note creates a related but slightly different problem, because it can be expanded to *and* or *ond* or kept as an abbreviation. Any of the choices has the potential to introduce artificial similarity or difference into the data. To solve this problem, we could through *lemmatization* convert all the notes and *and*s into *ond*s, the procedure that has been followed in other lexomic analyses of Old English texts.[4] However, in our analysis of *Beowulf* we were fortunate that the dominant form in the manuscript, Tironian note, had already been expanded by Klaeber to *ond* on a consistent basis, and that the few instances of *and* were sufficiently rare[5] that their conversion to *ond* or retention as the note had no effect on dendrogram geometries.

3.2   TEXT PREPARATION: EDITION AND TEXT

Even if the *Beowulf* manuscript had not been damaged by the 1731 Cotton fire and subsequent handling, the text would still need to be emended in order for us to read it. How much emendation is required, however, is controversial.[6] Previous lexomic analysis of Anglo-Saxon texts has been greatly facilitated by the availability of the high-quality *Dictionary of Old English* corpus, which uses the Anglo-Saxon Poetic Records editions of Old English poems, including Elliott Van Kirk Dobbie's 1953 edition of *Beowulf and Judith*.[7] But although Anglo-Saxonists have long been content with the ASPR editions of most other Old English poems, Dobbie's *Beowulf* is not the current scholarly standard. The 1953 text avoids many commonly accepted emendations and accepts manuscript forms rejected by most current scholars. Being conservative in emending a text can be a virtue, but previous lexomic research suggests cluster analyses based on critical editions are more reliable than those based on diplomatic texts.[8] We have therefore used our electronic version of the text of the fourth edition of *Klaeber's Beowulf and the Fight at Finnsburg*, edited by Robert E. Bjork, R. D. Fulk, and John D. Niles (hereafter abbreviated as KL4), since this edition is the most widely used and carefully scrutinized.[9]

Regardless of which edition we use,[10] the orthographic practices of the two scribes of the manuscript create some significant problems for computer-assisted analysis. As noted above, minor variations in orthography do not seem to affect cluster analysis substantially unless the variations are consistently distributed,[11] but such, unfortunately, is the case in *Beowulf*, which was copied by two scribes, A (lines 1–1939) and B (lines 1939–3182 and corrections of A's work). The differences in the scribes' orthography, particularly in their preferences for *þ* or *ð* and for *eo* or *io* spellings of diphthongs, are so consistent that almost all dendrograms simply divide into A-scribe and B-scribe portions of the text. Inspection of the table of ranked word frequencies for each group of segments indicated that this separation, although consistent with some hypothesized divisions of *Beowulf*, was likely an artifact rather than an actual separation in vocabulary distribution. Tellingly, *þis* ranked very highly in the A-scribe text, while *ðis* was correspondingly high-ranked in the B-scribe's portion of the poem: the consistent orthographic variation made it appear as if each scribe frequently used a different word when in fact the same lexemes were being employed.

There are two ways to avoid mis-identifying this consistent orthographic variation as variation in vocabulary distribution. First, we could examinine separately the A-scribe's and B-scribe's portions of the text. Such an approach can be (and indeed, was) effective, but by artificially dividing the poem at line 1939 it also limits the comparisons we could make. We therefore decided to work with a *normalized* version of *Beowulf* that would eliminate not only the scribal variation between <þ> and <ð> (which we could have eliminated via consolidation) but also the other consistent differences in spelling. We attempted to use Francis P. Magoun's 1959 normalized edition of *Beowulf*, in which the editor had converted the language of *Beowulf* into consistent early West-Saxon following the principles laid out in his 1956 *The Anglo-Saxon Poems in Bright's Anglo-Saxon Reader Done in Normalized Orthography*.[12] But, we discovered, Magoun's normalization was not entirely consistent and was done with a very heavy hand: not only was spelling normalized, but meaning was frequently changed. Additionally, Magoun's text is not perfectly comparable to KL4, since not only is it based on C. L. Wrenn's edition of 1958 but also includes, in addition to Magoun's own idiosyncratic emendations, "several" suggestions (not always identified in the text) that Magoun states were made by John C. Pope.[13]

We therefore produced our own minimally normalized version of KL4 that eliminated the differences between the scribes without making other changes to the text. We determined that, as long as spelling and orthography were internally consistent among repeated words, it was not necessary to force all the words in *Beowulf* to match an external standard in order to enable accurate and consistent cluster analysis. We therefore matched every word in KL4 to its corresponding lemma in the list created by Giuseppe Brunetti.[14] Wherever there was a difference in spelling among the tokens for a given lemma (i.e., *Beowulf* and *Biowulf*), we normalized the spelling of all of the subsequent tokens to be identical in root spelling to their first appearances in the poem, but we did not eliminate plurals or inflectional forms (i.e., *Biowulfes* was not lemmatized to *Beowulf* but merely normalized to *Beowulfes*). Although a fully lemmatized edition—such as the one produced by Brunetti—may be useful for some forms of analysis, previous research suggests that dendrograms produced from critical editions more closely match known controls. We therefore used our normalized critical edition (hereafter abbreviated as NormKL4) for some of the analyses discussed below. We have some confidence in this normalized edition because dendrograms produced from it of either the A-scribe or the B-scribe text in isolation are identical to those produced from the parallel sections of the un-normalized KL4. However, even though we are confident that the use of our normalized text does not of itself create artifacts in cluster analyses, we have used the un-normalized KL4 for those analyses which are contained entirely within one scribe's work and so would be unaffected by the consistent scribal differences.

Notes

1. Most text preparation can be done using software tools, but the removal of features like chapter headings, Roman numerals, Fitt numbers or footnotes must often be done by hand. Although the Lexos software suite has the capability of generating lemmatized texts, our research has not found any particular benefit to using these, nor have we found that results produced

from diplomatic editions are any more consistent with controls than those made from standard critical texts. For a detailed discussion see Boyd et al., 18–25.
2. Other abbreviations (such as those for *sanctus, episcopus* or *þæt*) are generally handled more consistently by editors and in any event are rare enough to have proven to be insignificant in all previous analyses.
3. Comparison among poems copied by different scribes often requires consolidation and lemmatization for *and, ond* and Tironian note. For example, the differences in the usages of *and/ond* between the Exeter Book and the Junius manuscript are so pervasive and consistent that they can overwhelm the similarities of vocabulary between *Azarias* and *Daniel*.
4. Consolidations changes every instance of a character string in the text whether or not that string is a stand-alone word or is part of another lexeme. Lemmatization changes only complete words.
5. Robert E. Bjork, R. D. Fulk and John D. Niles, *Klaeber's Beowulf: Fourth Edition*. Toronto: University of Toronto Press, 2008, 349.
6. See R. D. Fulk, "Textual Criticism," in *A Beowulf Handbook*, Robert E. Bjork and John D. Niles, eds. Lincoln: University of Nebraska Press, 1997, 35–53.
7. Elliott Van Kirk Dobbie, *Beowulf and Judith*. New York: Columbia University Press, 1953.
8. Boyd et al., 18–24.
9. Scholarly approval of KL4 is widespread but not universal. Kevin Kiernan's *Electronic Beowulf*, for example, presents an edition far closer to the manuscript text, and thus much closer to Dobbie's, than Klaeber's; Kevin Kiernan, ed. *The Electronic Beowulf.*, London: British Library, 1999. There are other editions available, ranging from Francis B. Magoun's *Beowulf* in normalized spelling to the diplomatic edition that accompanies the Zupitza facsimile; Francis P. Magoun, Jr., ed. *Béowulf and Judith*, revised by Jess B. Bessinger, Cambridge, MA: Harvard University Press, 1966; Julius Zupitza, ed. *Beowulf: Reproduced in Facsimile from the Unique Manuscripts British Museum MS. Cotton Vitellius A.xv*. 2nd ed. Oxford: Early English Text Society, 1959.
10. With the exception of Magoun's normalized edition.
11. If <þ> and <ð> are distributed randomly or generally evenly throughout a text, counting separately the words that use each form (i.e., counting *þat* separately from *ðat*) will not affect the Euclidian distance between segments, because the difference between the *thorn* forms in each segment will be added to the difference between *eth* forms: $(þ+ð)/2 = þ/2 + ð/2$. It is only when the *thorns* or *eths* are concentrated in particular segments that artifacts are produced.

12. Francis P. Magoun, ed., *Béowulf and Judith Done in a Normalized Orthography*, rev. ed. Jess B. Bessinger, Jr. Cambridge: Harvard University Press, 1959 [1966]. Francis P. Magoun, ed. *The Anglo-Saxon Poems in Bright's Anglo-Saxon Reader Done in Normalized Orthography*. Cambridge, MA: Harvard University Press, 1956 [1965], iv.
13. Magoun, "Foreword" *Béowulf and Judith*, [unpaginated].
14. Giuseppe Brunetti, http://www.maldura.unipd.it/dllags/brunetti/OE/TESTI/Beowulf/index.htm. Accessed 24 July 2014.

CHAPTER 4

Cluster Analysis of *Beowulf*

Abstract The initial results of hierarchical agglomerative cluster analysis of segments of *Beowulf* show a heterogeneity of vocabulary distribution. Techniques of screening, shifting and blending are used to identify robust segment boundaries. The text copied by the A-Scribe is analyzed separately from that copied by the B-Scribe, producing two "scrabble diagrams" of the similarities and differences among segments. The normalized text is then used to analyze the A- and B-Scribe texts together, identifying the boundaries of the segment divided between the two scribes and demonstrating similarities among segments in both parts of the poem.

Keywords *Beowulf*, scribes of • A-Scribe • B-Scribe • Scrabble diagram • Segment boundaries • Screening • Dendrogram • Lexomic methods • Normalization • Cluster analysis

4.1 Identifying Segment Boundaries: Screening

The complex, episodic structure of *Beowulf* and the lack of explicit scholarly consensus as to the boundaries of narrative units make it difficult to produce any single best segmentation of the poem.[1] Although there are fitt numbers in the *Beowulf* manuscript, these fitts vary significantly in size (with quite a number of them being smaller than the 500-word general threshold for cluster analysis), and their significance and relationship to the text are disputed.

The fitts, therefore, can not be used to divide the poem into obvious and uncontroversial segments, and the method of merely cutting the entire poem into segments of an arbitrary, round-numbered size—the procedure used in previous lexomic analyses of *Genesis, Daniel* and *Azarias, Guthlac A* and *B* and the Cynewulfian corpus—is not easily applied to *Beowulf*. By chance, both 1000- and 1500-word divisions split many episodes across multiple segments, for example, breaking *Beowulf's* fight with Grendel in two and thus putting each half of the battle into a different segment. In fact there is no single segment size greater than 750 words in which all of the resulting segments did not split up at least one obvious narrative unit. Dividing *Beowulf* into 1200-word segments, however, does avoid fragmenting most of the major episodes across multiple segments.[2] This arrangement is therefore a useful starting point that can then be used to screen for robust dendrogram geometries, which can then be further explored (Table 4.1).

We have found that a *ribbon diagram* of the poem (Fig. 4.1) can make segmentation of the text and interpretation of dendrograms significantly easier.[3] Such a diagram identifies divisions by word-count, line number, and narrative content, allowing us to match segment boundaries with the content of the text.[4] The ribbon diagram in Fig. 4.1 can therefore be used to interpret the dendrogram in Fig. 4.2, which shows the results of cluster analysis when *Beowulf* is divided into 1200-word segments using KL4.

We begin the interpretation of the dendrogram by reading from the top down, thus identifying the high-level clade structure. Cut into 1200-word segments, *Beowulf* separates into two major clades, α, containing segments 2, 3 and 9; and β, which contains the rest of the poem. β then sub-divides into γ (segments 10, 11, 12, 13 and 14) and δ, which further splits into ε (segments 4, 5, 7, and 8) and ζ (1 and 6). Because the divergence between α and β is the highest branch-point in the dendrogram, we can conclude that segments 2, 3, and 9; differ most in vocabulary from the rest of *Beowulf*. We also see a clear division within clade β between the end of the

Table 4.1 Line numbers for 1200-word segments of *Beowulf*

Segment #	1	2	3	4	5	6	7
Line #s	1–225b	225b–445b	445b–662a	662a–884a	884b–1112a	1112b–1323b	1323b–1541a

Segment #	8	9	10	11	12	13	14
Line #	1541b–1751a	1751b–1973b	1974a–2196b	2196b–2421a	2421a–2634a	2634a–2852a	2852a–3182

CLUSTER ANALYSIS OF *BEOWULF* 25

Fig. 4.1 Ribbon diagram of *Beowulf*

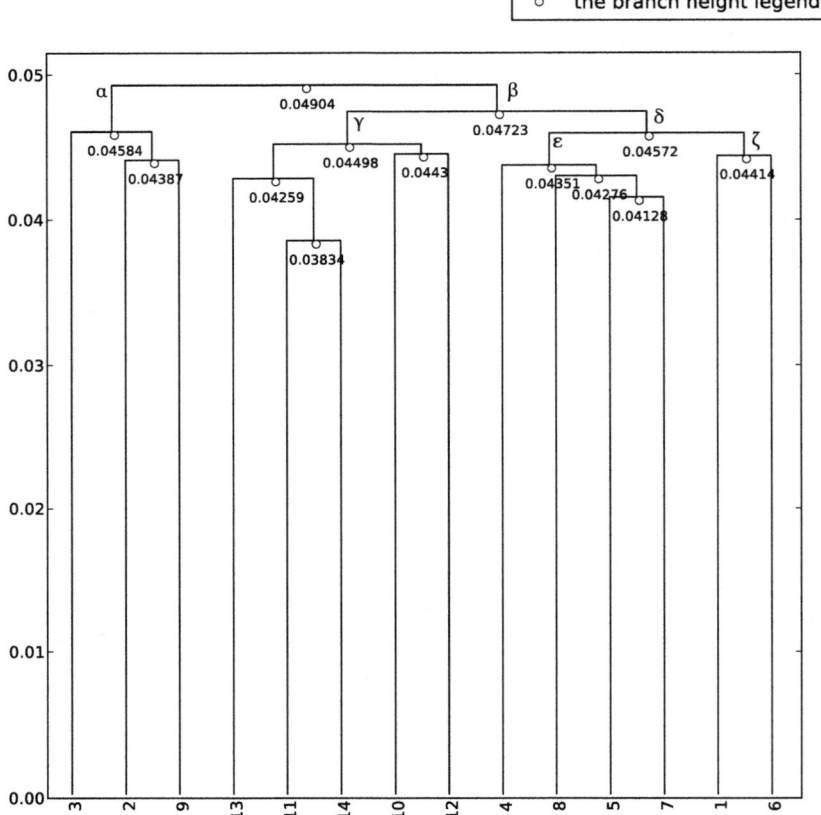

Fig. 4.2 Dendrogram of *Beowulf* KL4 divided into 1200-word segments

poem (segments 10–14) and the other parts of *Beowulf*. But, this division, although it does appear, in part, to map on to the traditional view of *Beowulf* as a two-part poem divided at either line 1888 or 2200, indicates one of the problems with using the un-normalized KL4 for cluster analysis: clade γ is made up entirely of segments copied by the B-scribe, and so we cannot have complete confidence that the division of clade β into γ and δ is based on vocabulary distribution rather than orthography. But despite this difficulty, the dendrogram in Fig. 4.2 is not entirely useless. For instance, the division between α and the rest of the poem cannot be based solely on orthography because while segments 2, 3 and much of 9 were copied by the A-Scribe, so were the segments in δ.

Clade α contains segments 2, 3, and 9, with 3 attaching to the pair of 2 and 9. Segments 2 and 3 extend from *Beowulf's* landing in Denmark through the end of the hall scene as Hrothgar turns over Heorot to *Beowulf* for the night, with the break between segments falling during *Beowulf's* speech declaring his intention to rid the hall of Grendel's attacks. Segment 9, which includes both A-Scribe and B-Scribe material, begins about two-thirds of the way through Hrothgar's Sermon (line 1751b) and extends through *Beowulf's* arrival at Hygelac's hall (line 1973). Clade β includes sub-clade γ, consisting of segments 10–14, the five segments that cover the Geatish portion of the poem and are all in Scribe B's hand (he takes over at line 1939, inside segment 9). Within γ, segments 11 and 14 form a pair with 13 attached, and this triad is linked to the pair of 10 and 12. As can be seen by the relative heights of their branch-points in the dendrogram, segments 11 and 14 are the most similar, forming a kind of envelope pattern, encompassing the opening and closing of the final section of the poem (segment 11 begins at line 2196b, nearly coinciding with the traditional division at line 2200). Segment 13, which attaches to the 11–14 pairing, includes the introduction of Wiglaf, the second phase of the dragon fight, and *Beowulf's* death. Segment 12 includes *Beowulf's* long speech recalling his life as well as the first phase of the fight with the dragon; this segment pairs with 10, which is *Beowulf's* recapitulation in Hygelac's hall recounting his experiences in Denmark. Both segments consist of a long speech by *Beowulf* recalling his past deeds and commenting on the actions of others.

The β clade also contains two other groupings, a pair (ζ) and a quartet (ε). The pair of 1 and 6 contains material external to the main narrative of *Beowulf's* adventures as well as an account of a monster attacking Heorot: segment 1 includes accounts of Scyld and others of Hrothgar's ancestors as well as Grendel's first incursions, while segment 6 includes the second half of the Finnsburg digression followed by Wealhtheow's speeches and Grendel's mother's attack on the hall. These two sections link with the quartet (ε) in which fights with monsters are prominent, with segment 5 pairing with 7 and 8 and then 4 joining on. Segment 4 is the entirety of the fight with Grendel (extending through the beginning of the Sigemund digression), while the fight with Grendel's mother is split fairly evenly between 7 and 8; segment 7 begins with Hrothgar's lament to *Beowulf* over Æschere's death, and 8 ends in the middle of Hrothgar's Sermon. Segment 5 begins in the middle of the Sigemund digression and extends through the first half of the Finnsburg digression. It is the only segment of the foursome that does not include a monster fight.

A number of patterns begin to emerge from this rough first approximation: the B-Scribe material clusters together, as do the Grendelkin fights. There seems to be a relationship between the Danish history in the early part of the poem (Scyld and his descendants) and the Finnsburg episode, and this material is distinct from the rest of the poem. Segments containing a high proportion of formal speech exchanges on arrival and departure also cluster together. Some of these relationships, however, are not as clear as perhaps they could be due to the frustrating tendency for any fixed-interval cut to divide episodes across multiple segments.

4.2 Identifying Segment Boundaries in the A-Scribe Text

To solve the problem of narrative units being divided, we can shift boundaries and identify robust relationships that persist across many different divisions of the poem. We can further align our segmentation with the underlying narrative by hinting the boundaries of segments. To avoid adjusting too many variables simultaneously, we will first examine the A-Scribe material, then the B-Scribe lines, and finally the entire poem.

4.2.1 *Finding Robust Geometries Using Shifting*

In order to correlate the boundaries of narrative units with those of our segments, we sought to identify particular geometries that persisted across multiple segment sizes, boundary locations and even between different editions of the poem. Shifting the boundaries between the A-Scribe segments by 300 words at a time, we examined the dendrograms thus produced for patterns that persisted through shifts of 300, 600 and 900 words. These robust relationships are potentially significant because they do not depend entirely on precise cutting or arrangement but appear to be caused by substantial underlying similarities or differences in the distribution of vocabulary in the poem. In the discussion that follows, we label these new, robust divisions arrived at via shifting with capital letters in order to keep them distinct from the numeric labels used in the 1200-word segmentation of Fig. 4.2.

The most robust dendrogram placements are those of segment C, which is often separate from every other clade of the poem, and of segments A and F, which are nearly always linked together and often separate from the rest of the text. These divisions can even be seen in our initial 1200-word screening: segment C corresponds reasonably well with segment 3 of Fig. 4.2 (although in the cutting arrangement used to produce Fig. 4.3, some of C had been left in segment 2), and the pairing of A and F pair corresponds, to a certain extent, with segments 1 and 6. Other clade placements are somewhat

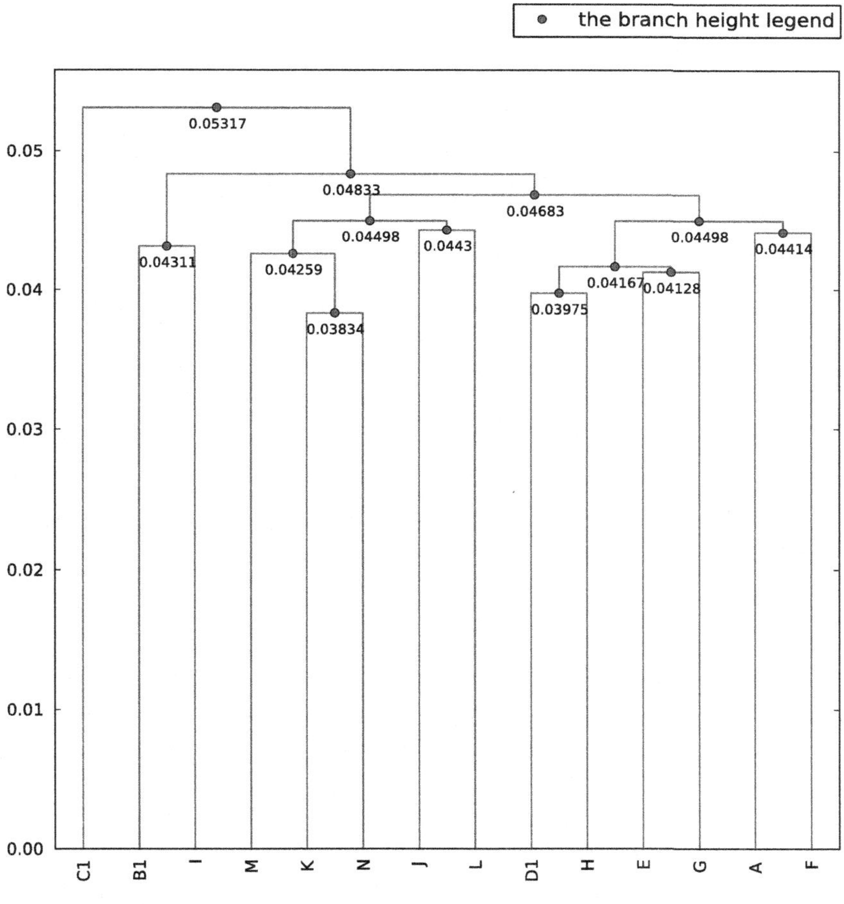

Fig. 4.3 KL4 segmented at 1200, segments C1 and B1 hinted to isolate the Unferth/Breca episode in C1

less robust, although we saw reasonable consistency in the linking of segments that contained *Beowulf's* fight against Grendel to segments that contained pieces of the fight against Grendel's mother. In multiple experiments, clades that contained these fight scenes stuck together, their proximity seeming to be related to the proportion of the monster combats that they contained. These variations in segment similarity demonstrate the greatest weakness of using a single segment-size in cluster analysis: the impossibility of choosing a single segment size that isolates potential sub-units of the text in natural boundaries. To address this problem, we began to move the boundaries of individual segments incrementally, using this process of hinting to match segments with logical narrative or rhetorical units of the poem.

4.2.2 Hinting Segment Boundaries

We began our process of hinting by placing the first division not at word 1200, but at word 1008, after line 188. This initial segment (A) includes the proem, the story of Scyld and Danish history up until the description of Grendel and the current Danish troubles. *Beowulf's* story, beginning with his journey to Denmark, thus starts at the beginning of the second segment (B). Our first experiments ended segment B at word 1971 (after line 370). Segment C thus began after Wulfgar's challenge and Beowulf's entry into Heorot, and continued until after the Unferth dialogue and the Breca story, concluding at word 3307 (line 606). Our many shifting experiments, however, had shown that any segment containing the Unferth and Breca material regularly appeared on a simplicifolious branch separate from the rest of the poem, while Wulfgar's challenge and the entry to the hall were consistently linked with the rest of segment B. We therefore hinted the boundary between B and C to preserve these two robust divisions, starting C (now C1) after line 489. This cut resulted in Hrothgar's first exchange with Beowulf and the promise to kill Grendel being moved from segment C to segment B (now B1).[5] These hinted boundaries produced the simplicifolious placement of the third segment (now C1) that had been so consistent in the geometries of the many dendrograms produced by the shifting experiments.[6]

4.2.3 Finding Robust Geometries Using Blending

Another robust pairing that emerged from our screening was between the monster fights in segments D, G and H. Segment D, which was made up primarily of the Grendel fight, and G, about fifty percent of which was Grendel's mother's attack on Heorot, regularly stuck together. However, lines 607–661, "Joy in the Hall,"—in which Wealhtheow enters the hall, greets the assembled troop and passes the cup—seemed to be causing conflicting results. When "Joy in the Hall" was part of D, that segment linked not with G, but with segment E. However, if we hinted the boundary between C and D to make "Joy in the Hall" part of C, then segment C became linked to E, with segment D returning to its pairing with G. If we moved "Joy in the Hall" to segment B, *that* segment then linked with E, C returned to being simplicifolious, and D and G were again connected. A large number of experiments showed that "Joy in the Hall" disrupts nearly all other robust geometries by causing whatever segment it is placed in to link with E. We conclude that "Joy in the Hall" is so like E in vocabulary distribution that its inclusion in any other segment makes that segment extremely similar to E in vocabulary, regardless of its other content.[7] "Joy in the Hall," therefore, seems to belong with segment E, and we can eliminate its distorting effect on dendrogram geometry by moving it to segment E1 through the process of blending.[8]

Once "Joy in the Hall" is moved to segment E1, the resulting segment D1, which begins with the warriors preparing for bed and ends with the Grendel fight, links to segment G. However, a complicating factor is the two-part nature of the fight with Grendel's mother, who attacks Heorot in lines 1251–1306a but does not fight Beowulf in her underwater lair until lines 1492–1622. Both G and H link to D1 depending upon the quantity of monster fighting in each of them. If we create a G that includes both halves of the fight with Grendel's mother, that segment links to D1 and H does not. If we create a segment that places one half of the fight with Grendel's mother in G and one half in H, both halves link to D1, and if we move both combats into H, that segment links with D1 and G does not. We therefore used blending in order to place all the fighting with Grendel's mother in a single segment. Both halves of the fight were moved to G1, and the non-fighting material (lines 1306b–1491 and 1623–1686) was moved to H1. The resultant dendrogram (Fig. 4.4, from which the B-Scribe clade has been removed for the sake of visual clarity) shows segment D1 linked to segment G1, demonstrating that the key elements in the 4, 5, 7, 8 clade in Fig. 4.2 were the two monster fights (which had been divided among those clades in the original 1200-word segmentation).

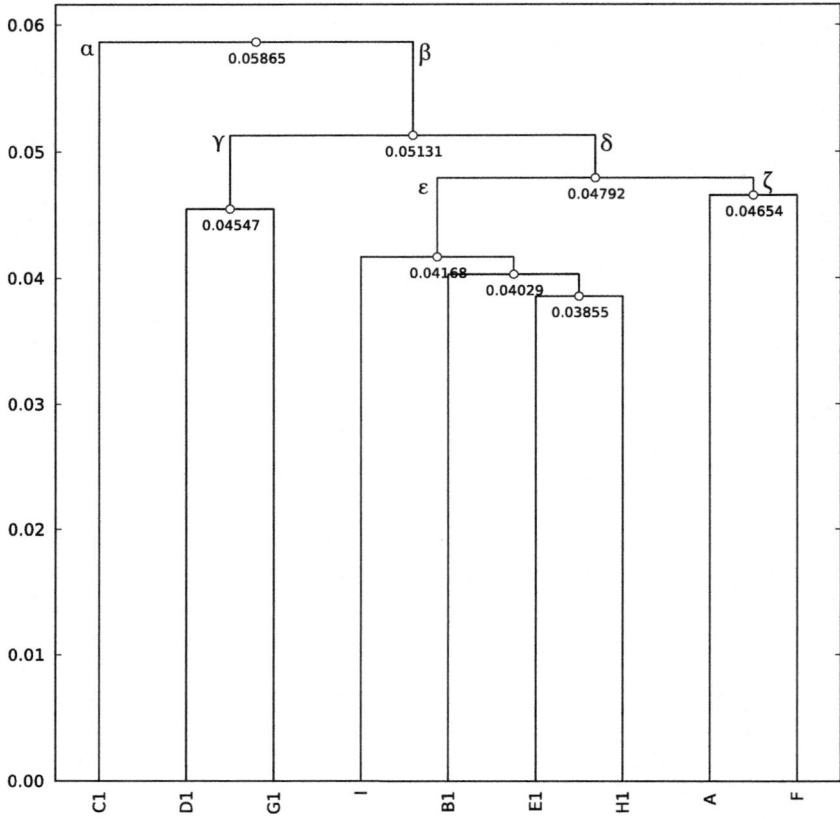

Fig. 4.4 KL4 hinted and blended A-Scribe material

4.2.4 Segment Boundaries for the A-Scribe Dendrogram

The remaining segment boundaries were largely forced by the choices described in the preceding discussion. The boundary between D1 and E1 is a logical narrative division between the end of the Grendel fight and the next morning in Heorot. The division between E1 and F and between F and G1 (line 1250) is placed so as to keep the entire Finnsburg episode within a segment. Segment I contains lines 1687–1887. Setting the boundary between this segment and J is difficult, as is the determination of the most logical boundaries for J. One termination point that keeps the segment close to 1200 words in length would be the departure of the Geats from Heorot (and that is what we have used in some analyses). Although Beowulf's journey back to Geatland could just as easily be part of this long narrative unit, including that material in segment I makes the resulting segment substantially longer than the other sub-units. However, including the return journey in segment J creates new problems, since the transition of the A-Scribe to the B-Scribe occurs after the return to Geatland but before Beowulf becomes king of the Geats. The evidence of underlying clade structure from the shifting and hinting experiments is less robust here, but in general B, I, E and H regularly stick together as a cluster. Segment J can link to this grouping as an outlier, but the geometries of the clades are highly sensitive to the placement of the divisions between I and J and between J and K. Because of the problem of the change in scribe and because any linkage of J to the rest of the segments is not robust under shifting and hinting, and because we did not want segment I to be so much longer than the other segments, we separated I from J after the departure of the Geats from Heorot at line 1887, a very traditional place to divide the poem. For now we exclude Segment J and the placement of the boundary between it and segment K from the discussion of the A-Scribe material, but we will analyze these in detail in Section 4.4.1.

We thus arrive at the arrangement given in Table 4.2. These divisions are a compromise between matching obvious narrative sections in the poem and creating segments that were reasonably similar in size. They correspond roughly with the numbered segments of Fig. 4.2, though there are some important differences. In Fig. 4.2, Beowulf's fight against Grendel was split among two segments (4 and 5), as was the fight with Grendel's mother (7 and 8). Most of the Unferth episode and Beowulf's Breca story were found in segment 3, but some was included in segment 2. Similarly, much but not all of the Finnsburg episode was found in segment 6.

Table 4.2 Segment boundaries in Fig. 4.4, KL4 A-Scribe, material hinted and blended

Segment	A	B1	C1	D1	E1	F	G1	H1	I
Lines	1–188	189–489	490–606	662–836	a: 607–661; b: 836–1062	1062–1250	a: 1251–1306a; b: 1492–1622	a: 1306b–1491; b: 1623–1686	1687–1887

4.2.5 Analysis of the A-Scribe Dendrogram

From these divisions we produce Fig. 4.4, a dendrogram which we believe to be the most accurate representation of the robust relationships among segments of the A-Scribe text. At the highest-levels of the dendrogram, the text divides into α, a simplicifolious clade that contains only segment C1; and β, which is made up of the rest of the text through line 1887. Clade β divides into two branches, the bifolious γ, containing only segments D1 and G1, and δ, which splits into four-leafed ε and two-leafed ζ. Clade ε is made up of clades B1, H1, E1 and I. Clade ζ contains only segments A and F. The *scrabble diagram* (Fig. 4.5) correlates distribution of vocabulary with line numbers and narrative content. Segment C, the dispute with Unferth and Beowulf's Breca story, is different in vocabulary from everything else in the A-Scribe portion of the poem. The next most distinctive sections of the poem are segments D1 and G1, the monster fights, which link to each other and whose branch is separate from the rest of the A-Scribe text. Segments B, E1, H1 and I are, as indicated by the stepwise geometry of clade ε, the most homogeneous segments of the poem. E1 and I are made up primarily of activity inside Heorot—speeches, colloquies and gift-giving. B and H1 also contain hall-related actions but are more focused on arrivals and departures. The pairing of A (the Proem and Danish history) and F (Finnsburg) appeared in dendrogram after dendrogram even though

Line Numbers / Content	1–188	189–455	456–606	662–836	607–661, 837–1062	1063–1250	1251–1306a, 1492–1622	1306b–1491, 1623–1686	1687–1887
monster fights				D1				G1	
hall business, arrivals, departures, journeys		B1			E1			H1	I
Danish history	A					F			
Unferth / Breca			C1						

Fig. 4.5 A-Scribe scrabble diagram

the clade is not always separated from the main body of the poem, indicating that these two segments are very similar to each other but not nearly as different from the rest of the sub-sections in the poem as the Unferth episode and not quite as distinct in vocabulary distribution as the monster fights. We withhold until Chapter 5 all comment on the possible significance of these relationships and proceed to a discussion of the B-Scribe portion of the poem.

4.3 Identifying Segment Boundaries in the B-Scribe Text

It should be emphasized that despite the complexity of the foregoing discussion, the A-Scribe material did in fact separate itself into relatively straightforward groupings since there were correlations between the robust clade-relationships and narrative or rhetorical subsections of the poem. It is more challenging to identify consistent recurrent patterns in the B-Scribe material, not the least because determining reasonable boundaries for segments of approximately 1000 ± 250 words is extremely difficult in this part of *Beowulf*. Almost none of the seemingly digressive elements in the B-Scribe portion of the poem are long enough to dominate a segment. For instance, none of the treatments of the past wars between the Swedes and Geats are as large as the single continuous Finnsburg episode; instead, these digressions are interspersed with other content in at least three main sections, and the fight with the dragon is divided up into multiple episodes separated by other material, only some of which is part of the main line of the narrative action. Furthermore, most of the more obvious potential sub-sections of this part of the poem are substantially smaller than our minimum segment size. Analysis of the B-Scribe text thus requires us to perform much more hinting, shifting and blending than was necessary for analysis of the A-Scribe material.

4.3.1 *Screening the B-Scribe Text*

In our initial screening of the poem, when we divided the entire text into 1200-word segments, we noted that the B-Scribe segments clustered together (see Fig. 4.2 above). Although tests with consolidated and normalized texts demonstrate that this separation from the rest of the poem is caused by the two scribes' different patterns of orthography and spelling, the arrangement of the segments *within* the B-Scribe text cannot be so influenced and is therefore potentially a useful first approximation of the structure of the final third of *Beowulf*.

The 1200-word whole-poem dendrogram (Fig. 4.2) suggests that there is both similarity among and difference between individual segments of the B-Scribe text. However, we are immediately faced with the problems associated with segment 9 (lines 1751b–1973), which contains material from both the A- and B-Scribes. If we create a segment J that ends at 1939a, where the scribal transition occurs, we subsume within the subsequent segment K the narrative break when the action jumps fifty years in only a few lines (2200–2209a), but if we separate J and K at 2209a, we retain some B-Scribe material in segment J. The only way to determine the affinities of the material in these lines and hence identify a robust boundary between J and K is to use the normalized text to eliminate the interference created by different and consistent orthographic practice of the scribes (which we will discuss below in §4.4). However, our present purpose is the independent analysis of the B-Scribe portion of the text using KL4, so we will start the first B-Scribe segment at line 1939b even though this is not an obvious syntactic, semantic or narrative division of the poem.

We begin by producing a screening dendrogram of lines 1939b–3182. Because the narrative units of this part of the poem seem to be smaller than those in the A-Scribe material, we used an initial segment size of 900 words, producing the dendrogram in Fig. 4.6.

The short vertical distances between branch-points in this dendrogram indicate that the text at this segment size is relatively homogeneous. There are two paired segments, and three simplicifolious clades arranged in a stepwise pattern. The most outlying of these, which contains the first 900 words in the B-Scribe portion of the poem, is somewhat different in vocabulary distribution than the rest of the text. After failing to identify any robust patterns through shifting, we deleted the first 100 words in the B-Scribe portion of the poem and then produced a new 900-word segmentation from which to generate a dendrogram. This process was repeated in 100-word increments until the entire initial 900-word segment had been deleted. We also performed this incremental deletion and analysis with segment sizes of 850, 950, 1000 and 1100 words.

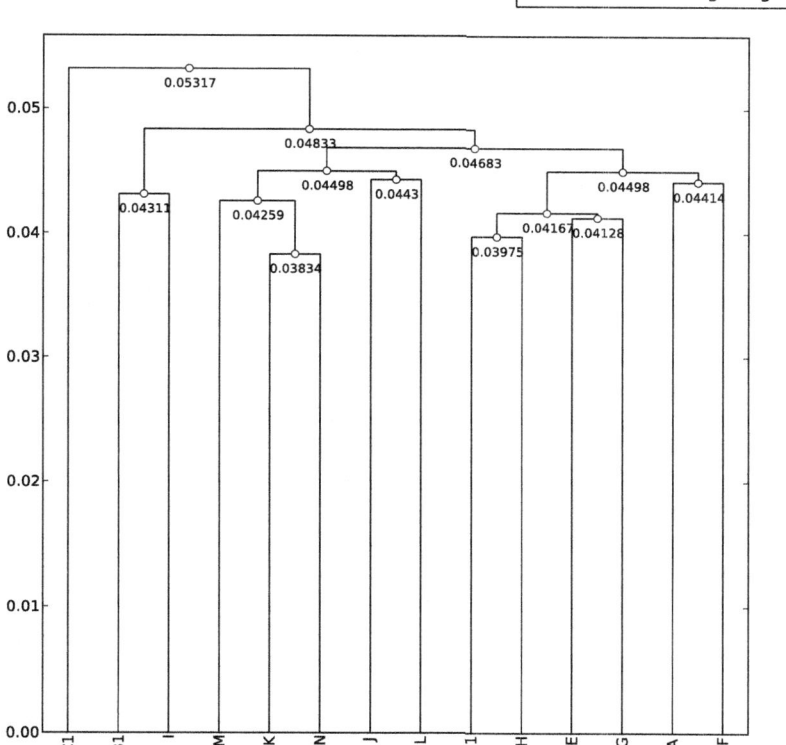

Fig. 4.6 Screening Dendrogram of lines 1939–3182 of KL4 in 900-word segments

4.3.2 Identifying Segments in the B-Scribe Text

Only two aspects of the many resulting dendrograms were particularly robust. First, the segment consisting of the initial 800–1000 words of the B-Scribe text is consistently simplicifolious in the dendrogram, indicating that it is substantially different in vocabulary than the rest of the text. The terminal boundary of this anomaly cannot be determined with absolute precision, but it seems to be within 200 words of line 2209a, when the time-frame of the poem shifts from Beowulf's youth to his old age.

We therefore begin segment K at this point, where narrative logic can be correlated with dendrogram geometry; lines 1939b–2209a are therefore excluded from the following analysis (we discuss them, and lines 1888–1939a in Section 4.4.1). Second, there exists a robust pairing between the material in lines 2279b–2354a and 2935–3182. The precise boundaries of this similarity are blurry, but the strongest pairings are between lines 2209b–2354a and the very end of the poem, lines 3028–3182. If we split a segment made up of words 1000–3000 at word 1500 and then augment the resulting half-sized segments with material from their neighboring segments, both new segments link with the end of the poem, indicating that it is the text from 2209b–2354a that has the greatest affinity with lines 3028–3182. Similarly, extending the final segment forward in the text to well before line 3028 does not change the geometry even when the clade becomes nearly twice its original size, indicating that it is the material after 3028 that has the affinity for the earlier segment. We therefore draw the boundary of segment K at 2354a and that of segment Q at 3028.

The many dendrograms we produced via shifting did not initially show other similarly robust patterns but instead indicated that the dendrogram geometries of the B-Scribe text were far more labile than those representing the A-Scribe material: the shapes of dendrograms could be significantly altered by relatively small shifts in segment boundaries, but all of the resulting dendrograms had stepwise geometries with very short vertical distances between branchpoints, characteristics that, in previous research, have been diagnostic of texts that are heterogeneous in vocabulary that have been divided into small sub-sections. Indeed simple examination of the text shows that this part of *Beowulf* does appear to be made up of shorter and more interwoven sub-units than lines 1–1887. Among the largest and most visible digressions from the main narrative are the "Lay of the Last Survivor" (lines 2247–2270), the deaths of Hygelac and Heardred (lines 2354b–2396), the "Father's Lament" (lines 2444–2462a), Beowulf's *beot* (lines 2510–2537), and passages relating to the death of Hrethel, the Geatish succession, and the wars between the Geats and the Swedes (2425–2443, 2462b–2509, 2892–3027). Unfortunately, these sub-sections are non-contiguous and too short to be hinted into independent segments; even the longest Swedish-wars digression at the end of the poem is only 620 words. Additionally, in many cases the location of the putative digressions within larger sub-sections prevented us from determining vocabulary similarity simply through the incremental shifting of boundaries. Blending was therefore required.

We began by making a blended segment that contained all of the dragon material, including the dragon finding the barrow and attacking the Geats in lines 2270b–2323, Beowulf fighting the dragon alone in lines 2538–2602, and with Wiglaf in lines 2669–2723. Results using this constructed segment were inconclusive. Depending upon the segmentation of the rest of the text, very different sub-sections of the poem linked with this "dragon blend," most frequently Beowulf's last words and death (2792b–2859). However, when that scene was itself divided across two segments, Beowulf's decision to attack the dragon (lines 2324–2354a) and his *beot* before the fight (2510–2537) were also paired with the dragon blend. Wiglaf's entry into the barrow (lines 2752–2792a) and his upbraiding of the cowardly retainers (2603–2668) also frequently connected with the dragon fighting. It eventually became clear that separating out the dragon fight was not clarifying the relationships among segments but was instead producing artifacts, perhaps because we were concentrating vocabulary that had affinities otherwise spread throughout the B-Scribe text.[9]

We therefore returned the dragon sections to their original locations in the text and instead gathered together the material about Geatish history and the Swedish wars, hinting the text so that the narrative of the deaths of Hygelac and Heardred (2354b–2396), of the Geatish succession and death of Hathcyn (lines 2425–2443), and Beowulf's defeat of Dæghrefn and revenge for Hygelac (lines 2462b–2509) were all in a single segment. This Geatish history blend paired up with a segment comprised of the messenger's telling of the Swedish wars and the story of the death of Ongentheow (lines 2892–3027). Both of these segments are quite short (respectively 710 and 620 words), so although the pairing so created was relatively robust, we can not be entirely certain that the linking of the segments is not an artifact. However, in previous research, very short dissimilar segments have tended to be arranged in single-leafed clades separate from all other segments rather than pairing with each other, supporting the conclusion that the linkage of Geatish History and the Swedish Wars identifies the boundaries of segments L and P and their similarity to each other.

If we divide the B-Scribe text along these lines (setting aside the material in segment J), we generate a reasonably robust dendrogram. Segment K begins with the 50-year time shift and ends with Beowulf's decision to attack the dragon. It is paired with segment Q at the end of the poem, which starts with the disposal of the dragon and the preparations for the funeral. Both of these segments include descriptions of funerals and buried treasure. The next pairing is between the short segments L (lines 2354b–2509) and

P (2892–3027), which are made up primarily of Geatish history. Segment L includes the Geatish succession, the Father's Lament, the death of Dæghrefn and Beowulf's revenge for Hygelac (as will be discussed in §4.4.2, the presence of the Father's Lament in this segment creates some additional problems). Segment P is comprised of the messenger's explanation of the Swedish wars, the death of Ongentheow and the predicted disasters that will befall the Geats.

We are now left with the three clades that contain Beowulf's combat against the dragon. Segment M is straightforward, composed as it is of contiguous material, lines 2510–2668, that contains Beowulf's *beot* and his initial battle with the dragon as well as the introduction of Wiglaf, who upbraids the cowardly retainers before the battle. Segments N and O are somewhat more complex, because a short section of O, lines 2860–2891 in which Wiglaf criticizes the retainers after the battle, behaves very much like "Joy in the Hall" (discussed above in §4.2.2): the placement of these lines in any dragon- or history-related clade causes that clade to link with segment N. We therefore move these lines from O to N, producing new segments N1 and O1. N1 contains lines 2669–2751, in which Beowulf and Wiglaf fight the dragon together before Beowulf is wounded and the two warriors exchange words, and also Wiglaf's chastising of the retainers in lines 2860–2891. Segment O1 is made up of Wiglaf's examination of the barrow and Beowulf's last words and death (2752–2859). However, segment O1, when it is shortened by the removal of lines 2860–2891, now becomes simplicifolious. By additional hinting and blending, O1 can be made to link to M and N1, but such integration of the dragon fighting clades seems to be caused in great part by the inclusion of the N1 material that has such a powerful effect on the geometry of the B-scribe dendrogram. We are therefore caught between creating a somewhat artificial link between N and O or making O so short that it moves into a simplicifolious clade in the dendrogram.

The most robust of the segment linkages in the B-Scribe text can be represented as a scrabble diagram (Fig. 4.8). We note that funerals and buried treasure (K and Q) bracket Geatish history (L and P), which frames the battle against the dragon and Beowulf's death (MNO). Excluding segment J, the B-Scribe material begins with the death of the last survivor and the dragon's occupation of the barrow, moves into a section focused on the Geatish history that explains Beowulf's being king, and then develops the core of the narrative: Beowulf's fatal defeat of the dragon. A second section of Geatish history explains why Beowulf's great feat does not lead to peace and prosperity for his people but rather the opposite, and then the poem ends with the funeral of the hero and the interment of the treasure. This is a classic envelope pattern.

CLUSTER ANALYSIS OF *BEOWULF* 41

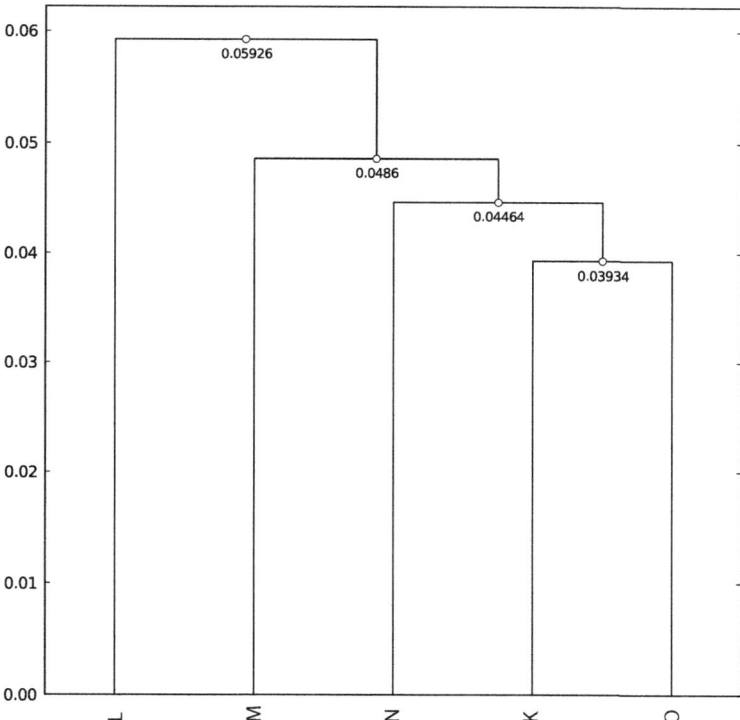

Fig. 4.7 KL4 B-Scribe text after hinting, segment J excluded

Line Numbers Content	2209b- 2354a	2354b- 2509	2510- 2668	2669- 2751, 2860- 2891	2752- 2859	2892- 3027	3028- 3182
funerals and buried treasure	K						Q
dragon fighting			M	N1	O1		
Geatish history		L				P	

Fig. 4.8 B-Scribe scrabble diagram

4.4 Analysis of the A-Scribe and B-Scribe Texts Together

Having constructed the most robust dendrograms possible from the A-Scribe and B-Scribe texts separately, we can now use our self-normalized text of *Beowulf* to see how the material from lines 1–1887 may relate to that in lines 1888–3182 once the effects of scribal performance are eliminated.

Figure 4.9 is the result of segmenting the normalized text precisely at 1200 words. Comparing this representation with that produced from the un-normalized text, we note both similarities and differences. In the dendrogram of the normalized text, although the B-Scribe material is no longer isolated, some of the relationships noted in the un-normalized text are not disrupted: segments 6 and 1 still cluster together, and a stepwise cluster of 3, 2 and 9 remains separated at the highest level of the dendrogram (although 10 now joins these three segments). The grouping of 5 with 7 and 8 also remains, but in the normalized text, 13 is part of that cluster while in the original screening it was 4 that was included. Segment 4 is now, with 11 and 14, part of a trifolious clade. In sum, the previous B-Scribe clade has partially dissolved, with segment 13 seeming to switch places with segment 4 and segment 12 moving to an outlying location in clade β. The affinities of the segments are broadly similar to the original screening, and the material from the final third of the poem appears to have some connection with the monster fights in the earlier portion: Beowulf's initial fight against the dragon joins the Grendel's mother material, while the Grendel fight is similar in vocabulary to both the dragon's attack and its subsequent defeat by Beowulf and Wiglaf.

Figure 4.9, however, is based on an un-hinted, un-blended text that does not take into account the robust boundaries and relationships that we have identified from shifting, hinting and blending the text in each scribe's portion of the poem. When we produce a normalized text that matches those divisions, we see a somewhat different dendrogram geometry (Fig. 4.10), in which segments L, O1 and P are simplicifolious outliers to a bifolious main division of the poem into clade η (segments N1, Q, K, D and G) and θ (the rest of the poem). Within η, we find a single-leafed outlier (segment C1) and two major divisions, clade μ, which contains the robust pairing of A and F, and the large stepwise clade ν that contains segments M, I, B1, H1, E1, and J.

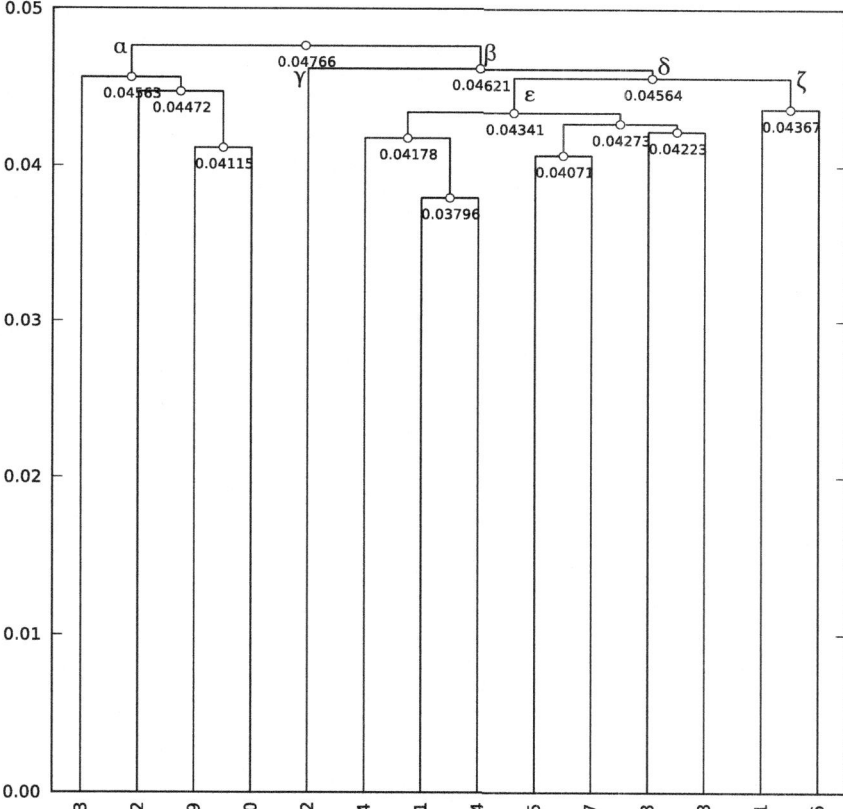

Fig. 4.9 Normalized KL4 in 1200-word segments

Figure 4.10 demonstrates some of the difficulties in comparing segments of disparate size. Because all three of the outliers are extremely short in comparison to the other segments, we cannot, from the dendrogram alone, determine whether there is a substantial difference in vocabulary distribution between segments L, O1 and P and the rest of the poem or if their dendrogram placement is merely an artifact of their small size; previous research suggests the latter, as does the analysis of the B-Scribe segments of the poem alone. In that analysis, segment L linked with P, and O1 was part of the weakly connected M, N1, O1 grouping. To attempt

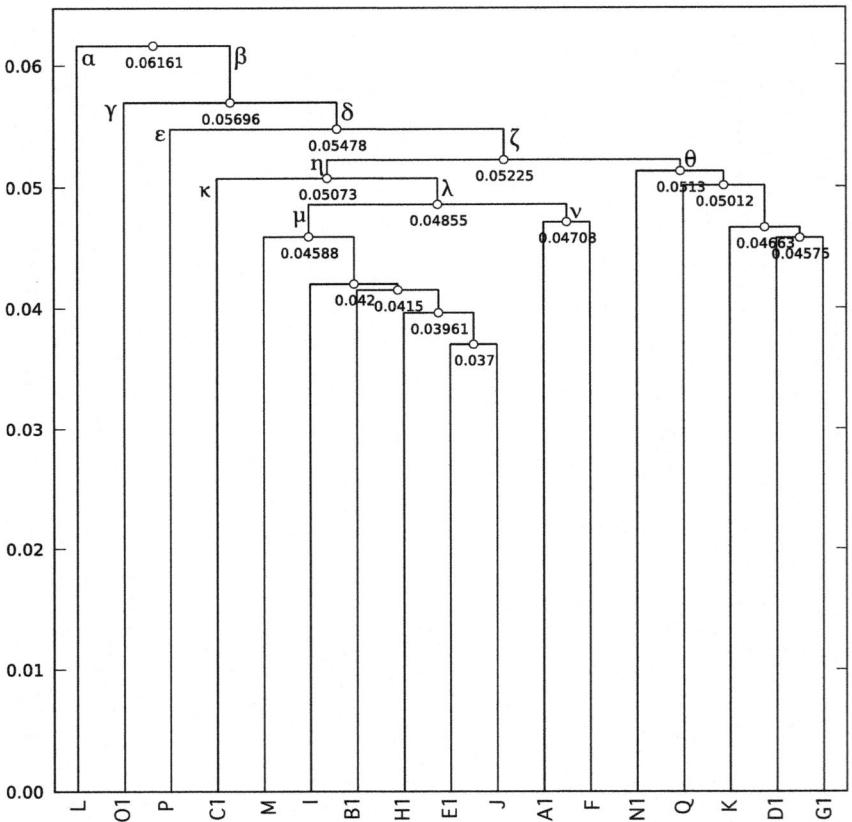

Fig. 4.10 Normed KL4 after hinting and blending

to eliminate the short-segment artifacts, we combined segment L with segment P to produce a single, larger segment, the content of which was Geatish history and the Swedish wars. This composite segment (L&P) became part of clade λ, the extremely robust pairing of segment A (the proem) with F (Finnsburg). The merging of L and P further affected the dendrogram by changing the placement of other B-Scribe clades, with N1 moving from clade θ to a simplicifolious placement in the dendrogram (it is not entirely clear why N1 shifts clades, since L and P were not part of clade θ in Fig. 4.10). The rest of Fig. 4.11 is consistent with the separate

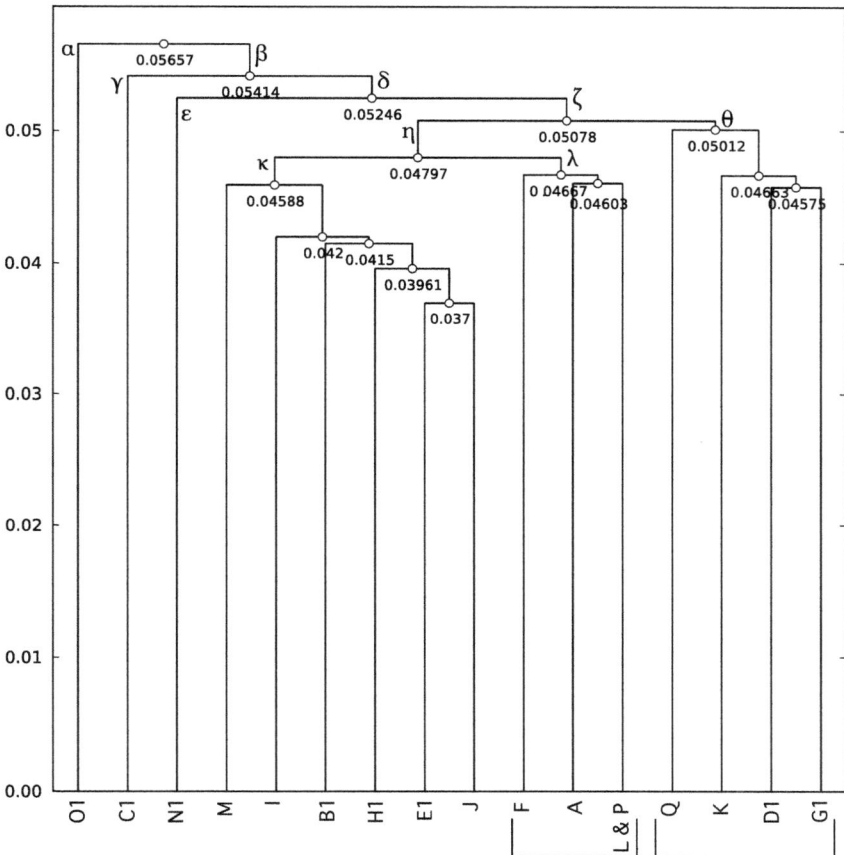

Fig. 4.11 Normed KL4 after hinting and blending, segments K and P merged

analyses of the A- and B-Scribe portions of the text but show affinities across the scribal boundary: in addition to the linkage of the combined L and P segments with A and F, segments K and Q, containing funerals and treasure, are linked with D1 and G1, the Grendelkin fights.

To see if the placement of M, N1 and O1 was also an artifact of small segment-size, we merged these three segments (Fig. 4.12). Merged M, N1 and O1 becomes part of the large, stepwise clade μ, but other relationships in the dendrogram are now disrupted: segments K and Q move

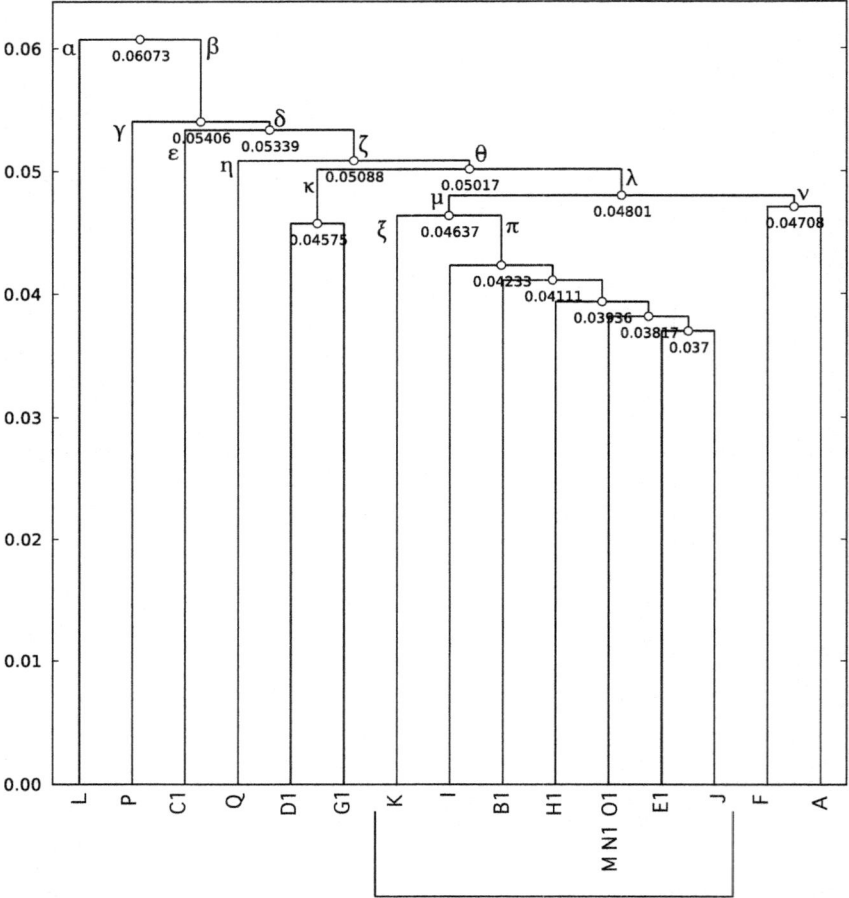

Fig. 4.12 Normed KL4 after hinting and blending, segments M, N1 and O1 merged

out of the clade with D1 and G1 and become single-leafed outliers within clades, while L and P are outliers in the entire dendrogram. If we also merge L and P, this segment moves from being paired with A and F to become part of the large central clade. We infer that, while merging clades can eliminate the artifacts caused by very short segments, the process creates new problems because the merged segments become more like each other in an artificial homogeneity. We therefore conclude that it is not possible to produce what our research group called the "one true dendrogram" of *Beowulf* but that instead we must rely on cross-comparison of multiple dendrograms to identify robust relationships among segments.

Nevertheless, we can extract some meaningful information from Figs. 4.9–4.12, noting that patterns that we saw in the separated, nonnormalized texts remain in the complete normalized text. When it is not in the same segment as Beowulf's arrival in Denmark, the Unferth and Breca material in segment C1 again has the most distinctive vocabulary distribution in the entire poem. The rest of *Beowulf* then divides between a group in which every segment at least mentions monster fighting, and everything else—a cluster which is itself divided between the very robust pairing of the proem with the Finnsburg episode and the remainder of the poem. The shifting, hinting and blending experiments show that links between the B-Scribe material and various A-Scribe segments are less robust than those among the A-Scribe segments, but that there are some consistent patterns. The Geatish history and Swedish Wars segments (L and P) have a tendency to link with the proem and Finnsburg (A and F). Segments K and Q (funerals and treasure) tend to link with the monster fights (D1 and G1), and segments M, N1 and O1 (primarily dragon fighting) appear to fit into the large B1, E1, H1, and I grouping, as does segment J.

4.4.1 Segment J

The consistent differences in orthography between the two scribes has to this point prevented us from establishing a firm boundary between segment J and its neighbors, I and K. A screening exercise in which we slightly hinted the boundary between I and J many times until the dendrogram geometry shifted led us to conclude that the traditional division of the poem at 1887 was consistent with the vocabulary distribution, but because this boundary was solely within the text copied by the A-Scribe, we could not easily separate J and K. However, when we use the self-normalized text to analyze the entire poem, we find that both the linkage of J with the E1, H1, B1, I clade and the geometry of this grouping is strongly influenced by where we set the boundary between J and K. The further the boundary is moved past line 2209a, the less tightly the resulting segment sticks to the four-part clade in the A-section of the poem and the more likely it is to link with clade Q. If we divide J in half, J_1 remains somewhat similar to E1, H1, B1, I, while J_2 moves towards the outside of the dendrogram and becomes simplicifolious,[10] indicating that it is the first part of K rather than the second half of J that is similar to Q and further supporting the division, based originally on our analysis of the B-Scribe text alone, that the separation between J and K occurs near line 2209a. If we incrementally shift the boundary between J_1 and J_2, we find that the largest separation between the two sub-segments occurs if we divide between 2069a, when Beowulf has finished telling Hygelac about Freawaru and the Heathobards, and 2069b, which begins Beowulf's retelling of his adventures in Denmark. This separation indicates some underlying heterogeneity in the vocabulary of J, but if we were to split the section at this point, both resulting segments would be less than 1000 words (J_2 would be only 736 words). However, excising just the story of Freawaru and the Heathobards from J does not cause the segment to be any more tightly integrated into the E1, H1, B1, I clade. We conclude, therefore, that the boundaries of segment J should be set at 1888 and 2209a, but that the segment itself is, even in the normalized version, only weakly linked to either half of *Beowulf*, though it is more like the earlier part of the poem in vocabulary than the later.

4.4.2 Blending and Deleting to Determine In-Clade Relationships

The resolution of any single dendrogram is limited by the minimum segment size of 750–1000 words. Simple inspection of the ribbon diagram (Figure 4.1) strongly suggests that even a many-segmented dendrogram cannot hope to illuminate all of the relationships among sub-sections of *Beowulf* because some of these narrative units, although they are smaller than 750 words, nevertheless perturb dendrogram geometries. A series of experiments suggested that among the most influential of these narrative units are the "Lay of the Last Survivor" (lines 2247–2270), the deaths of Hygelac and Heardred (lines 2354b–2396), the "Father's Lament" (lines 2444–2462a), Beowulf's *beot* (lines 2510–2537) and the messenger's explanation of the Swedish wars and the future doom of the Geats (lines 2892–3027). The presence or absence of these sub-sections is almost never sufficient to shift a segment out of the high-level clade in which it is normally found, but changes in their placement can modify the internal geometry of clades.

To tease out the inter-relationships among these sub-segments and to attempt to understand their influence on the larger scale dendrogram geometries, we undertook a long and complex program of hinting, blending and deletion from which certain patterns emerged. First, material about history and politics, primarily about the Danes (most importantly the story of Freawaru and the Heathobards) but also including the account of Offa and Thryth, clusters with the A-F grouping (Danish history and Finnsburg). Second, the Grendelkin fights (D1 and G1) are more similar in vocabulary to the beginning and end of the B-Scribe portion of the text (K and Q) than they are to the three central dragon-fight segments (M, N1 and O1), no matter how much we subdivided and re-arranged the latter segments. Finally, sub-sections focused on Geatish history and the wars between the Geats and the Swedes link with the A-F cluster but they also have some affinity with segments K and Q.

The similarity of segments A and F and their separation from the other material in the largest clade of the dendrogram is an extremely robust result of our cluster analysis. Segment A contains historical background about the Danes, including the proem and its account of Scyld; the Finnsburg episode makes up most of segment F. This material, in particular the Finnsburg episode, has often been identified as being digressive from the main narrative of the poem. To see if other putative digressions would, if separated from the text that surrounds them, link to the A-F pairing, we created artificial segments that gathered together the major digressions. Into segment X we placed the account of Offa and Thryth (1920–1962), the description of Freawaru's imagined future (2020–2069a), the Lay of the Last Survivor (2231b–2277), and the Father's Lament (2425–2471). Segment Y contained all the material on the wars between the Geats and the Swedes (2354b–2396, 2472–2509, 2900–2998). In the dendrogram produced from this particular arrangement, segment X is linked to the pair of A and F (proem and Finnsburg), and segment L (the Geatish succession) links with D1 and G1 (the battles with the Grendelkin). To this grouping attaches Y, the account of the Geatish-Swedish wars. The rest of the post-J material from the poem, segments K, M, and N1, attach weakly to the core of the A-Scribe segments associated with actions in the hall, arrivals and departures (E1, H1, B1, I). This clustering seems to indicate that some of the "digressions" have similar vocabulary distributions to segments A and F. Swapping around the various subsections from the X to the Y clade produced no robust patterns in the geometries of the resultant dendrograms. The Geatish history and Swedish wars segments do in some configurations connect with A-F, particularly when the Thryth or Freawaru digressions are included in Y, but they have nearly as much affinity for the segments of the poem containing the dragon's attack and Beowulf's funeral and did not consistently link with the main narrative of the two-part dragon fight. It is also possible to produce a clade comprised entirely of monster fighting (D1, G1, M, N1, O1), but this requires the deletion of most of the influential sub-sections of the final third of the poem: The Lay of the Last Survivor, the dragon's attack, the Geatish succession and The Father's Lament. We therefore conclude that the dragon-fighting scenes themselves are slightly less similar in vocabulary distribution to Beowulf's fights against the Grendelkin than they are to the E1, H1, B1, I clade.

From this complicated blending and hinting we get some idea of the relationships among smaller sub-sections of the poem, but the interwoven nature of the text, the size of the segments and the intrinsic limitations of cluster analysis make any conclusions much more tentative than our larger cluster analysis. It does seem as if there is a reasonably strong similarity between some of the other historical materials (Thryth and Freawaru) and the A-F segment, and somewhat less strongly connected to these segments is the material about Geatish history and the wars with Sweden. However, the latter also has similarities to segments K and Q. These segments themselves are also linked to the monster fights (D1 and G1), but neither the individual elements nor the grouping as a whole is particularly similar in vocabulary to Beowulf's fight against the dragon.

4.5 Synthesis of Cluster Analysis of Beowulf

The scrabble diagram in Fig. 4.13 represents a synthesis of all the cluster analyses of *Beowulf*. Features within the A- and B-Scribe sections of the poem are mostly unchanged, but now we see similarities of vocabulary distribution at a higher level of the dendrogram hierarchy. From this diagram we can identify three large-scale, multi-segment groupings and two outliers. Segments D1, G1, K1 and Q1 contain the fights against the Grendelkin, the dragon's attack, the Lay of the Last Survivor, and Beowulf's funeral. B1, E1, H1, I, M, N1, O1 are a fairly homogeneous grouping that contains arrivals and departures and happenings in the hall (in the first half of the poem) and the two-part fight against the dragon in the second (which includes more formal speeches than the segments containing the Grendelkin fights). Segments A and F are tightly paired and then linked with moderate strength to L and P, creating a clade of historical and political material whose first half is associated with the Danes and whose second depicts the Geats and the Swedes. Segment C1, the Unferth and Breca material, is dissimilar from all other segments in the poem. Segment J,

CLUSTER ANALYSIS OF *BEOWULF* 51

Line Numbers / Content	1-188	189-455	456-606	662-836	607-661, 837-1062	1063-1250	1251-1306a, 1492-1622	1306b-1491, 1623-1686	1687-1887	1688-2209a	2209b-2354a	2354b-2509	2510-2668	2669-2751, 2860-2891	2752-2859	2892-3027	3028-3182	Content
monster fights				D1			G1				K						Q	funerals and buried treasure
hall business, arrivals, departures, journeys		B1			E1			H1	I	J			M	N1 O1				dragon fighting
Danish history	A					F						L				P		
Unferth / Breca			C1															Geatish history

← recapitulation

Fig. 4.13 Full poem scrabble diagram

which is composed primarily of Beowulf's recapitulation of his adventures in Denmark, is not as distinctly different as C1, but like that segment, it is only loosely similar to the very large homogenous clade that contains hall business, arrivals and departures, and the dragon fights. Even these hinted and blended segments, however, are somewhat heterogeneous, with particular sub-sections in some of them having vocabulary distributions distinct from their surrounding matrices. The Thryth and Freawaru segments may be similar to segments A and F, but determining the affinity of the Lay of the Last Survivor, the Father's Lament, and, surprisingly, the Geatish succession, requires techniques beyond cluster analysis.[11]

Notes

1. Even among strongly opposed critics, there is much more general agreement about narrative boundaries than might be expected. See Yvette Kisor, "Numerical Composition and *Beowulf*: A Reconsideration," *Anglo-Saxon England* 38 (2009): 41–76.
2. The fight with Grendel's mother is not preserved in this particular segmentation, and the Finnsburg episode, Hrothgar's sermon and the dragon fight are similarly divided between more than one segment. However, the 1200-word division preserves the integrity of more of the major episodes than any other single-sized-segment division of the poem. Note that the overall size of the poem forces the final segment of the 1200-word division to be somewhat larger (1764 words) than the rest of the segments.
3. To the best of our knowledge, ribbon diagrams were first devised by Michael D. C. Drout and Courtney LaBrie in 2011. These visual representations are independent of and distinctly different from the ribbon diagrams (also known as Richardson diagrams) used in chemistry and biology for the representation of protein structure.
4. The amount of information that can be included in a printed ribbon diagram is limited by production requirements. For a very large and much more elaborated ribbon diagram of *Beowulf*, see http://beowulfribbondiagram.org
5. When we further hint the segment boundaries beyond the locations identified by shifting we append a number to the segment label. Thus segment B1 is the hinted version of segment B.
6. That C1 is simplicifolious could simply be caused by its small size. However, the Unferth and Breca material remains an outlier even if we combine it with substantial parts of other segments to make the segment 1200 words long. The one exception was when the segment contained the "Joy in the Hall" material discussed in section 4.2.3.

7. For additional discussion of this section of the poem see Michael D. C. Drout and Leah Smith, "A Pebble in the Stream of Tradition: 'Joy in the Hall,' (Lines 607–661 in *Beowulf*)" [forthcoming].
8. Because the ribbon diagram must be arranged according to the order of the text, we append lower-case letters to the segment label in order to indicate that non-contiguous material has been placed together in a single segment for the purposes of cluster analysis. For example, Grendel's mother's attack on Heorot and Beowulf's combat against her in her underwater cave are labeled, respectively G1a and G1b.
9. The color metaphor is again helpful as an intuition pump: if the text were composed of small strips of red, blue and yellow, larger segment sizes could produce purple, green or orange segments whose similarities could therefore be substantially perturbed by only very small changes in boundaries.
10. It is not, however, separated as far from the rest of the poem as C1.
11. The Sigemund digression, the two discussions of Heremod and the *Brisinga mene* material are all too short or entangled with surrounding material for effective cluster analysis.

CHAPTER 5

Interpretation of the Cluster Analysis

Abstract Lexomic methods indicate several robust groupings of segments in *Beowulf*, both within each scribe's portion of the text and in the poem as a whole. The most distinctive findings are that segment C, the Unferth/Breca episode, is substantially different in vocabulary from every other segment of *Beowulf*. Segments A and F (the "proem" on the Scylding dynasty and the Finnsburg episode) are highly similar to each other and distinct from the rest of the poem, with the exception of segments L and P, both of which contain Geatish and Swedish history. Segments D and G, containing the fights with Grendel and Grendel's mother, are similar to each other but not similar to the segments that contain the dragon fight. These results show at the least the presence of distinct discourses, most likely caused by the poet's use of multiple sources. Consistencies between the A- and B-scribe sections do not strongly support the hypothesis that the two sections have different authors.

Keywords *Beowulf* • Unferth • Breca • Finnsburg episode • Scylding dynasty • Proem • Scyld Scefing • Geats • Swedes • Grendel • Grendel's mother • Dragon • Wiglaf

Thus far we have deliberately avoided linking particular observations to traditional arguments about *Beowulf*. This reticence on our part may seem perverse to some readers, but our determination to present all the

© The Editor(s) (if applicable) and The Author(s) 2016
M.D.C. Drout et al., *Beowulf Unlocked*,
DOI 10.1007/978-3-319-30628-5_5

evidence before drawing conclusions is grounded in our experience. We found that it was extremely easy to jump to conclusions in the first flush of excitement about lexomic results, seizing upon a single piece of evidence that appeared to support one side or another in the major debates about *Beowulf*. Such premature interpretation often set back the larger project, as the full implications of the data were for a time suborned to the narrow original judgment. This tendency was further exacerbated by the remarkable tradition of *Beowulf* studies, in which almost every line of the poem has been analyzed in great detail. This accumulation of scholarship is an intellectual monument, but its existence can hamper our ability to identify and explain larger-scale features of *Beowulf*. Arguments that assiduously pause to explicate the previous work on each word or line are often so turgid that their implications escape even specialists. The combination of the new methods, the contentious current debates, and the scholarly tradition can produce a narrow and tendentious focus that undermines one of the strengths of the new methods: their potential to detect patterns of similarity or difference that are distributed across a text. We have therefore reserved our interpretation until this section of the paper, and even here we focus primarily on *de minimis* conclusions.

5.1 Groupings of Segments

Cluster analysis demonstrates that *Beowulf* contains multiple segments whose vocabulary is distinctively different from each other. Many, but not all, of these segments link in groupings that are not based entirely on either rare or function words (although the latter are more influential than the former). The relationships indicated by the scrabble diagrams, therefore, are not merely the result of similar events being described in different parts of the narrative.

5.2 High-Level Similarities and Differences

Beowulf contains three groups of mostly similar segments and two outliers that are distinctively different from the rest of the text. The largest but also most diverse group is composed of segments B1, I, E1, H1, which links across the scribal divide to M, N1, and O1, with these last three being somewhat more tightly liked to each other and less closely connected to the earlier group of four. Segments E1 and H1 are predominantly composed of material related to the interactions of warriors in the mead hall.

Feasting, dialogue and speeches make up the majority of the two segments. Segments B1 and I are similarly focused on warriors, but these two sections of the poem are dominated by descriptions of journeys, departures and arrivals. To this group join the three segments that contain Beowulf's and Wiglaf's battle against the dragon. Although there is obviously much action in this section of the poem, it is tightly interwoven with speeches and descriptions of the social interactions of warriors, material broadly similar to that in segments E1 and H1. Note that the dendrograms of this large group usually have the stepwise geometry characteristic of relatively homogeneous texts. For convenience we can call these segments the *hall group*.

Segments D1 and G1, which contain the fights against the Grendelkin, are linked to each other. They are less robustly connected to K and Q from the final third of the poem, segments which each contain a funeral (the Lay of the Last Survivor and Beowulf's funeral) and references to treasure being buried. Although segment K does include the dragon's initial attack, there is no fighting at all in Q. Furthermore, segments M, N1 and O1, which contain the two-part battle against the dragon, do not link strongly to this grouping, indicating that the similarity of the segments is not due to their containing depictions of combat. We label D1, G1, K and Q the *monster and treasure group*.

The single most robust pairing in the cluster analysis is between the historical background of the Danes (segment A) and the Finnsburg episode (segment F). This connection does not appear to be based entirely on style, since the first segment is primarily a summary of kingly history while the second is a single episode presented in detail.[1] The linkage between this pairing and segments L and P, which contain the history of the Geats and their wars with the Swedes, is somewhat stronger than that between the dragon fight and the A-scribe portion of the hall group. We label A, F, L and P the *historical group*, subdivided into Danish and Geatish history. We should note that there are smaller segments spread throughout the poem that also may link (at least weakly) to this group, the most important of which are the Thryth digression and Beowulf's proleptic story of Freawaru and the Heathobards.[2]

Finally, there are two segments, C1 and J, that are not similar to the rest of the poem. The separation of C1 from all other segments in *Beowulf* is a very robust result of the analysis, perhaps only comparable in strength to the pairing of A and F. Beowulf's confrontation with Unferth and his story about the swimming match with Breca do not seem on their surfaces to be fundamentally different than other interactions in the hall, but the vocabulary distribution of this *Unferth segment* is extremely distinctive.

Segment J is not quite as different from the rest of the text as is C1, but its vocabulary is distinct, a finding which is perhaps surprising, given that the majority of the segment is the re-telling of the narrative in the poem up through line 1887. Depending upon its boundaries, this *recapitulation* can link to the very large and homogeneous hall group, but its non-robust positioning indicates that it is not particularly similar to any of the other segments, though it is somewhat more like the A-I portion of Beowulf than it is like K-Q.

5.3 INTERWOVEN DISCOURSES

Segments of *Beowulf* do not cluster together solely in terms of content or of style, though both seem to contribute (if only by proxy) to the heterogeneous distribution of vocabulary. The consistency within the clusters and the differences among these groupings allows us to identify them, at minimum, as *discourses*, overlapping but distinct subsets of a language-tradition. Our analyses identify the five discourses (discussed above), which are woven together throughout the poem. *Beowulf* begins with the *historical* discourse, in which is introduced the background of the Danes and their struggles with Grendel. It then shifts to the *journey* subset of the *hall* discourse, as Beowulf travels to Denmark, engages with the Coast Guard, proceeds to Heorot and speaks with Hrothgar inside that hall. The *Unferth* discourse begins in the hall but then switches to the events outside: first Unferth's and then Beowulf's relating of the swimming match against Breca. Other, brief *hall* business ("Joy in the Hall") separates the end of the Unferth discourse from the beginning of the *monster treasure* discourse, in which Grendel attacks and Beowulf defeats the monster. A segment of *hall business*, interspersed with short bits of *historical* material (the Sigemund and first Heremod digressions), and the *historical* discourse then becomes dominant during the Finnsburg episode told by the court poet in Heorot.

In Grendel's mother's attack on the hall, the reaction, the journey to the mere, Beowulf's fight with the monster, and subsequent action in the hall, we see an intercutting between the *monster treasure* and *hall* discourses, with the latter predominating in the material up through line 1887 although the primarily *hall* material at the end of H1 is replaced by a *journey* discourse in segment I. The *recapitulation*, in some ways its own discourse, in others related to the *hall* material (perhaps because Beowulf tells his tale while in Hygelac's hall), is a transition between the two primary settings of the poem, Denmark and Geatland. Within the recapitulation segment there are examples of *historical* discourse: the Thryth and Freawaru digressions. The poem then returns to the *monster treasure* discourse for the Lay of the Last Survivor and the dragon's attack. The *historical* discourse that follows explains the Geatish succession and thus how Beowulf became king. This section includes the Father's Lament, although it is difficult to be certain that this material is indeed part of the *historical* discourse.

Beowulf's interaction with his retainers, his *beot* and initial fight against the dragon, then Wiglaf's introduction, his speech to the retainers and his joining the hero in his battle, and finally Beowulf's last words and death are, in terms of cluster analysis, all of a piece and therefore potentially of a single discourse more closely related to the *hall* than to the *monster treasure* material. We must note, however, that in these segments the poem is so tightly interwoven between scenes of combat and scenes of speaking that it is difficult to separate these into different discourses. In some sub-divisions of the poem, the fighting is linked to the *monster treasure* discourse, but this is often not the case. After Beowulf's death the *historical* discourse is used in the explanation of the wars between the Geats and the Swedes. The poem concludes with Beowulf's funeral in the *monster treasure* discourse.

There are also some larger-scale patterns of the distribution of discourses in *Beowulf*. If we exclude the Unferth discourse, we see a nested envelope pattern or chiasmus in the first third of the poem (up through Finnsburg): historical, hall, monster treasure, hall, historical. This pattern has fewer levels in the second third of the poem, with hall material being interleaved with the fights against Grendel's mother. Wealhtheow's speeches and the Danes' preparations for bed are followed by the attack of the monster, which is separated from Beowulf's underwater battle by speech in the hall, the journey to the mere, and Beowulf's promise. After Grendel's mother is defeated, the narrative returns to the hall for Hrothgar's reading of the sword hilt, his sermon and then, after a night without monster attacks, gift-giving. The departure from Denmark and the journey to Geatland close out this section of the poem in the *journey* subset of *hall* discourse that is parallel to segment B. Segment J, the recapitulation, separates all of this material from the more pronounced envelope pattern in the final third of the poem, in which monster treasure discourses (K and Q) surround historical discourses (L and P), which in turn surround the mixed hall and battle discourse of the two-part dragon fight (M, N1 and O1).

We identify these patterns of discourses from examining *Beowulf* alone, correlating the results of the cluster analysis only with our general and somewhat abstract reading of the narrative content of the poem. This level of interpretation does not go beyond the poem itself; we have not chosen boundaries or labels so as to link the groupings and their relationships to hypotheses about the sources, composition, structure or authorship of *Beowulf*. In so doing we have explicated the discursive structure of *Beowulf* without, to this point, discussing possible causes of the poem's heterogeneous distribution of vocabulary.

5.4 Sources

Beowulf has presented greater challenges for cluster analysis than other Anglo-Saxon texts. But as we have addressed the problems of scribal variation and textual heterogeneity, we see no good reason to disregard the knowledge previously gained from lexomic analysis of Old English poetry and prose. Some patterns of discourse arrangement in *Beowulf* could perhaps be special-pleaded away as simply arising from the poem's narrative; for example, differences between the vocabulary of events in the hall and battles with monsters might simply be an epiphenomenon of the linguistic differences between direct speech and rapid action or between speech and summary.[3] It is difficult, however, to explain all the features of the vocabulary distribution solely in terms of variations in the content of the underlying narrative. There is no obvious reason why *Beowulf* should not behave similarly to other Old English poems in which major clade boundaries are consistently correlated with sources. The simplest hypothesis that accounts for all of the data is that some sections of *Beowulf* have difference sources than others. Although this interpretation was for many decades a fundamental assumption (even a conclusion) of *Beowulf* scholarship, it has been strongly disfavored in a post-Tolkien critical climate that has celebrated the poem's artistic unity.[4] But the conflation of the artistic unity of the poem with a putative lack of immediate sources is an error in logic, and both the accumulation of small pieces of evidence[5] and the larger patterns shown by the lexomic methods indicate that *Beowulf* had more than one immediate source.

5.4.1 *Unferth and Breca*

The placement of segment C1, the Unferth and Breca material, as an absolute outlier in nearly all dendrograms of *Beowulf* does not appear to arise from any obvious difference in either content or style between this material and the rest of the narrative. All the features of C1 are found elsewhere in the poem: dialogue between Beowulf and Unferth is analogous to that between Beowulf and a number of other characters, including the Coast-guard, Wulfgar and Hrothgar, and Beowulf's narration of the Breca story is not obviously qualitatively different than his recapitulating his fight against the Grendelkin. We must therefore seek some other explanation for the distinct difference in vocabulary distribution between this segment and the rest of the poem.

In previous lexomic research, it has been found that those segments of a poem that have different sources cluster separately from each other.[6] In cases where only one segment is based on one source but the rest of a poem is based on another or has no external source, segments appear as outlying clades,[7] so the many dendrograms in which C1 is simplicifolious are consistent with the Unferth and Breca material having a different source than the rest of *Beowulf*. This idea was proposed long before the advent of lexomic methods by Rudolf Koegel, who in 1894–1897 argued that there had been an old lay recounting the swimming match.[8] Summarily rejected by R.W. Chambers in 1912,[9] the notion was revived in arguments by Larry D. Benson in 1970 and Alistair Campbell in 1971 and given further support by Carol Clover ten years later.[10] Benson argues that Unferth's introductory statement in line 506 "Eart þu se Beowulf, se þe wið Brecan wunne" [are you the Beowulf, he who contended with Breca?], indicates the existence of an early poem—which the poet would have assumed his audience to have known—in which Beowulf lost the swimming contest. Beowulf's telling of the story, then, is an effort "to explain away this embarrassing bit of legendary history."[11] Campbell's suggestion that the episode derives from an archaic lay is based on very different and separate evidence: the unusual usages of "reon" (512), "þehon" (513) and "ford" (568), which Campbell sees as arising from an archaic written source.[12] Clover assembles comparative material that strongly suggests that disputes in verbal duels are based not on the invention of new stories but on "real" references.[13] Bjork, Fulk and Niles label lines 499–661 "the Unferð Intermezzo," and note the presence of "an unusually prominent capital letter (of *H*, given the scribe's understanding of the name)" in the manuscript at this point, but they dismiss the idea that an earlier text underlies the passage on the highly subjective grounds that "the story of the swimming exploit is not very promising material for a lay."[14]

Promising or not, four separate streams of evidence combine to support the idea that the Unferth and Breca material has a source different from the rest of *Beowulf*: the dendrogram geometry that is diagnostic of an external source; the archaic usages identified by Campbell; Benson's literary-critical judgment that it would be awkward for Unferth to say "the Beowulf, he who" if the audience did not already know that version of the story; and Clover's comparative analysis that a shared story often underlies a *flyting*. That the four types of evidence are independent of each other is a strong point in favor of the interpretation that a separate text containing the Unferth and Breca material existed before *Beowulf*.[15] However, the lexomic evidence could also be consistent with the notion that C1 is a later addition to *Beowulf* with a cleverly written transition at line 506 that implies an audience's knowledge (even if that audience never possessed such information). At the very least we can say, without yet taking a position on the priority of either segment C1 or the rest of the poem (or whether the source of the segment was a written text or an oral poem), that it is likely that C1 has a source *different* from that of its surrounding matrix.

5.4.2   Finnsburg and Danish History

As noted above, one of the most robust relationships in all of our analyses has been the pairing of A and F and their separation from the main body of the text. Once we have shaken off our unease about considering the possible influence of external sources,[16] we find no difficulty in hypothesizing the existence of a textual version of the Finnsburg episode that antedated *Beowulf* as we have it. The mere existence of the Finnsburg fragment demonstrates unequivocally that more than one version of the story existed, in written form, in the Anglo-Saxon period.

Because there is no definitive evidence that either the episode or the fragment derives directly from the other, many scholars have concluded that they are both based upon an earlier version of the story. The precise relationship of this hypothesized antecedent to *Beowulf* has been hotly debated, as has the putatively oral or written nature of the source. Bjork, Fulk and Niles casually dismiss the notion that the episode could be in itself a separate lay "inserted" into *Beowulf*,[17] attributing that conclusion to "the early dissectors" as well as to Campbell.[18] In their discussion they espouse what is probably the mainstream opinion of contemporary scholars: that if the poet "has drawn on such sources in framing the digressions, almost every one of them demands the conclusion that he has reworked the material thoroughly and in original ways."[19] But regardless of the precise relationship between the fragment and episode, both must have an ultimate common source. The presence of a few unusual and lexically similar words in the fragment and episode—*eorðcyning* and *eorðbuend*, *hildeleoma* and *swurdleoma*—does not prove that the common source was written,[20] though perhaps these words do imply a tradition that was interlinked and relatively stable even beyond the level of plot.[21]

Lexomic analysis is not inconsistent with the interpretation that the material in *Beowulf* is "reworked" from whatever its source was. The sections of *Genesis A*, *Guthlac A*, *Daniel* and *Juliana* that have previously been identified lexomically as having differing sources were very much "reworked" by their authors when they were translated or adapted from existing texts. Cluster analysis does not demonstrate that a separate lay was inserted into *Beowulf*, only that at this point in the composition the author had a different source for the material than that of the text outside of the segment. In this sense the findings about segment F are almost a control result: they replicate knowledge we had already acquired through other, more traditional methods. But although cluster analysis can identify the influence of a different source, it gives us no direct information about the specific characteristics of that source. Either a written text (poetic or prose) or an oral traditional poem could affect the geometry of a dendrogram. All we can detect from the methods alone is that segments A and F are different from the rest of the text but similar to each other.

If the existence of a source for the Finnsburg episode is an unexceptional conclusion, the same cannot be said for the implications of the linkage of segment A (lines 1–188) with F. Beginning with Ludwig Ettmüller in 1840, the critical tradition had taken the opening lines of the poem as being separable from the rest of the text on the grounds that the content of these lines "stands in no necessary connection with the poem itself."[22] Of particular concern to Ettmüller and the scholars who followed him was the lack of any connection between the Danish "Beowulf," the son of Scyld, and the hero of the poem.[23] This particular discrepancy is eliminated with the widely accepted emendation of "Beowulf" to "Beow" in line 18a,[24] but it was not the sole basis for the conclusions of nineteenth-century scholars that this section of the poem had a different source. In 1869 Karl Müllenhoff asserted that "it seems beyond doubt to me that the introduction [lines 1–193] was composed neither by the poet of the first old lay nor by one of the continuators or interpolators." Müllenhoff based this conclusion not only on the seemingly dropped thread of a Danish king named Beowulf, but also on the failure of Hrothgar's daughter (whose name has been lost in the lacuna at 62) or his brother Halga to be referenced later in the poem where their names and ancestry would be relevant.[25] Müllenhoff and many other proponents of *Liedertheorie* also sought to remove any putative Christian material from the poem, so other passages of segment A, including the "creation hymn" (lines 92–100a) and the passage about the Danes worshipping idols (lines 175–88), were also interpreted as arising from a different source or author. However, as Bjork, Fulk and Niles note, since the early part of the twentieth century the opening lines, particularly 1–52, have been "accepted as a deliberate part of the poem's design,"[26] and although lines 175–188 have long been suspected to be an interpolation, contemporary scholarship has not hypothesized a source for the rest of the text in segment A.

Cluster analysis is not affected by the presence or absence of few proper names, so the many dendrograms in which A is linked to F are not simply a reflection of the particular bits of information upon which Ettmüller, Müllenhoff and others based their evaluations. Furthermore, the passage from line 175–188 is too small to have significantly perturbed the geometry of the dendrogram, and in fact, the A-F pairing is retained even if lines 175–88 are deleted from the segment. The lexomic methods, therefore, appear to be suggesting an external source based on evidence—the distribution of the whole range of vocabulary—that is entirely independent of that used by previous scholars who reached the same conclusions.

Remarkably, this conclusion was anticipated more than half a century ago by J.R.R. Tolkien, whose notes on *Beowulf* were only published in May 2014, more than two years after our research group first identified the pairing and separation of segments A and F. "I think that in all this early part of *Beowulf* our poet is sticking very close to some old material *already in verse*; hardly doing more in parts than work it over," Tolkien wrote.[27] Unfortunately, he did not provide a sustained argument for the existence of this earlier written source, although it is possible to piece together some of his reasoning from the notes on a number of individual lines. For example, Tolkien asserts that lines 106–114, in which the poem describes the origins of monsters, are "an *insertion* or *addition*. Not an interpolation; that is, they seem to me to bear the impress of the style, rhythm and thought of the 'author'. Yet they do interrupt the simple sequence of narrative—and syntax."[28] Such an authorial insertion into passages that were being re-worked implies, Tolkien believes, the existence of an earlier poem about matters in "the 'Arthurian' court of Heorot, glorious and doomed, gnawed already by the canker of treachery."[29] As it stands, the argument is not much more than a hunch,[30] but the hunches of a philologist and scholar of Tolkien's calibre are worth considering, particularly if they are consistent with other evidence independently derived. That segment A is not only separated from the rest of the poem but is linked with segment F is additional support for the hypothesis of *Beowulf* having a textual source for this early part of the poem. A textual version of the Finnsburg story undoubtedly existed at some point, and both segments A and F are concerned with the background of the Danes. Additionally, the tendency of other Dane-focused digressions to link to segments A and F—in particular Beowulf's discussion of Hrothgar's doomed alliance with the Heathobards—could be evidence that there once existed a poem (or poems) about Danish history and politics that was known to the author of *Beowulf*.

The influence of such a poem on *Beowulf* could also in part explain the seeming inconsistencies that so troubled scholars from Ettmüller and Müllenhoff to Magoun but have been mostly explained away by modern critics. The purposes of a poem about the Danish court are not *Beowulf*'s purposes, and so the emphasis (or lack thereof) on various characters, events and relationships would have been different. Such a poem would be more like the Ingeld epic that Alcuin chastised the monks of Lindisfarne for enjoying in the refectory and which W.P. Ker wished the *Beowulf-poet* had written instead of *Beowulf*.[31] It would contain much information about Danish history, politics and dynastic relationships, which the author of *Beowulf* would have at his fingertips, until the narrative of *Beowulf* departed from the source, from which point names, kinship relationships and other details that were less relevant to the main storyline could easily be left out. Indeed, many of the discrepancies that were most significant to the older scholars turn out to be variations in detail and emphasis rather than actual contradictions in content.

We have here another confluence of various independent streams of analysis: the results of the lexomic methods, Tolkien's hunch, and (more speculatively) Müllenhoff's and others' contention that important information in segment A is not taken advantage of in later sections of the poem. The core conclusions of each line of reasoning would be harmonized if indeed the author of *Beowulf* had a source for segment A as he did for segment F, and this conclusion is not actually inconsistent with the widely held opinions of many scholars that the opening lines of the poem are an integral part of *Beowulf*'s overall structure and design,[32] that, as Helen Damico has remarked, "the proem *is* a digression."[33] A poet's choosing to "re-work" material does not necessarily imply that the material is not part of his artistic purpose or is unimportant for the rest of the poem. Quite the contrary: the deliberate selection and modification of a source text can indicate that the poet thought that the material thus chosen was important indeed. External sources have been identified for the Fall of the Angels in *Genesis*, the hellmouth episode in *Guthlac*, God's speech to the damned souls in *Christ III* and the Song of the Three Youths in *Daniel*, yet these sections are dramatically, emotionally and intellectually essential to those poems. It is not difficult to make the case that the externally sourced material is often the core of an Anglo-Saxon poem.

Cluster analysis strongly suggests that both the beginning of *Beowulf* (lines 1–188) and the Finnsburg episode have a different source than either the Unferth and Breca episodes or the rest of the poem. Unfortunately, the methods by themselves cannot tell us whether or not such sources were oral or written, prose or poetry, Old English or another language. Nor can we, from the lexomic analysis alone, determine definitively if segments C1, A and F are older or younger than the main text of *Beowulf* or if they are later insertions into an already existing text or sources for the text's original composition. All they can tell us on their own is that the segments are *different* in vocabulary distribution from the body of the poem and that A and F are more like each other than they are like any other segment. Techniques discussed in the follow-up monograph to the current study may help resolve some of these questions, as can the correlation of the lexomic results with evidence established through traditional approaches.

5.4.3 *The Fights with Grendel and Grendel's Mother*

The segments containing Beowulf's battles against the Grendelkin (D1 and G1) clustered with each other and separately from the rest of the poem almost as frequently as did A and F. But although we intuit that the influence of an external source is less likely for these sections of the poem than it is for the Danish historical material, it is difficult to identify objective reasons why the poet could not have had sources for these segments. Indeed, there is an old and vast scholarly tradition arguing that the Grendelkin material has sources in everything from Scandinavian texts like *Grettis saga* and *Hrólfssaga kraka*, to classical and biblical works, to folktales such as "The Bear's Son Tale" and "The Hand and the Child."[34]

The assumption that the poet must have had a source for the monster fights was so dominant throughout the first century of *Beowulf* criticism that even as late as 1932 Alois Brandl was moved to ask, exasperatedly: "should we not for once make the experiment of understanding the cannibal and the fire-breathing dragon as the original layers, with the historico-geographical setting understood only as a later disguise?"[35]

If scholarship has not carried out Brandl's exact experiment, it has moved away from inferring the existence of a written source. The dominant critical position for some years has been that a folktale pattern of "The Bear's Son Tale" in its "Two-Troll" variant underlies both *Beowulf* and *Grettis saga*.[36] Although the advent of oral traditional scholarship somewhat complicated this notion,[37] oral theory did not significantly alter the scholarly belief that any source for the story of the fights with Grendel and his mother was unlikely to be textual. Our own reluctance to entertain the possibility of a source for the monsters may be the lingering effects of the reaction, exemplified by Brandl, of the interpretive community of *Beowulf* scholars against previously dominant ideas. It is also likely conditioned in part by the enduring power of Tolkien's arguments in "*Beowulf*: The Monsters and the Critics."[38] For more than a scholarly lifetime—perhaps since W.P. Ker, and certainly since Tolkien's 1936 lecture—the monsters have defined *Beowulf*.[39] Accepting, even temporarily and for the sake of argument, the possibility that the poet had a source for them therefore moves against some of the strongest currents of modern scholarship. But in fact the existence of a source does not have to be interpreted as moving the monsters out of the center of *Beowulf*. As noted above, the influence of a source does not require us to believe that the sourced content was unimportant to the poet or the poem: it may indicate just the opposite.

We therefore should not reject out of hand the hypothesis that the *Beowulf*-poet had a source for the monster fights in Denmark. The cluster analysis indicates that the material in D1 and G1 has a different distribution of vocabulary than the rest of the poem and, as noted above, previous research suggests that these sorts of differences in vocabulary distribution are diagnostic of differences in sources. Although cluster analysis itself cannot tell us if a source was written or oral, it is difficult to see how a consistent difference in vocabulary, divided over two segments that are separated from each other by dissimilar material, could be sustained if all the poet was using was the plot outline taken from a folktale. Consistency in vocabulary between segments implies the existence of a formally stable source, whether oral traditional or written. Stability in form is also implied by the odd detail that the word *hæftmece* (hafted-sword) in *Beowulf* is paralleled with *heptisax* (hafted sword) in *Grettis saga*. The two words may indeed be reflective of "the long arm of coincidence,"[40] but the presence of the parallel *eorð-* and *–leoma* compounds in the Finnsburg episode and fragment suggests that similar processes of influence may be at work in this part of the poem as well and that we have in these segments the re-working by the author of *Beowulf* of pre-existing material.

Both Larry D. Benson and Anatoly Liberman concluded that *Beowulf* and *Grettis saga* have a common source that explains their similarities, but, unfortunately, the characteristics of their hypothesized sources are incompatible.[41] Tolkien also thought that the author of *Beowulf* was re-working older material for Beowulf's fights against the Grendelkin. In the notes on *Beowulf* published in 2014 (which were most likely written in the 1930s), Tolken argues that underlying the story of the fights against Grendel and his mother is a folktale related to "The Bear's Son Tale," first identified as a potential source by Panzer. Tolkien reconstructs this story in his charming *Sellic Spell*, in which the character Beewolf and his companions Handshoe and Ashwood fight against the monster Grinder, who has been troubling the King of the Golden Hall. Handshoe and Ashwood are killed by the monster, but Beewolf wrenches off Grinder's arm. Then, assisted by the king's councillor Unfriend, he tracks the fatally wounded beast to his lair and there defeats the monster's mother.[42] Tolkien's reconstruction is appealing but also extremely speculative, and it is probably wise to resist his remarkably powerful rhetoric.

There are, however, some reasons—beyond those of ideology, filial piety or critical tradition—to hesitate before interpreting the similarity in vocabulary between segments D1 and G1 as indicating that they have a common external source. First, it is important to remember that the linkage between D1 and G1 is only as strong as that between A and F when we use the technique of blending to bring together the attack on Heorot by Grendel's mother and Beowulf's battle against her in her lair in segment G1, thus isolating these sub-sections of the poem from the more hall- and warrior-related material (which is moved to segment H1). If the author of *Beowulf* did use a written or formally stable oral source rather than just a remembered plot for this section of the poem, then he cunningly interlaced the sourced material with a great deal of his own invention or from another source. It is not impossible that an Anglo-Saxon poet could do such a thing, but while we have examples of the addition of source material to poems, we have no such evidence of the kind of detailed weaving together of multiple *written* sources that such a hypothesis would require. Against this conclusion, however, we have the evidence of *Beowulf* itself. As the ribbon diagram (Fig. 4.1) shows, the entire poem is a complex blending of discourses. Indeed, lexomic methods were not required to recognize the interlaced structure of *Beowulf*.[43] If the poet was able to knit together material that was disparate but entirely of his own composition (the default assumption of contemporary criticism), then there seems to be no overwhelming logical objection to finding him inter-weaving words from a written source with that of his own invention.[44]

More substantial is the problem of the links (albeit weaker ones) between the D1 and G1 pairing and other segments of the poem. Although the core dragon-fighting segments do not link very strongly to the Grendel fights, they do, in certain configurations, connect to them. However, this linkage is less robust than other connections, and to the best of our knowledge no one has ever proposed that the two fights in Denmark *and* the dragon material could have been drawn from a single external source. Furthermore, segments K and Q link to D1 and G1 even more consistently than M, N1 and O1, and it is difficult to imagine a single external source that would include both of the fights against the Grendelkin and the paired funerals-and-buried-treasure material that brackets the final third of the poem. Taking all of this complex evidence into account, the case for an external source for this cluster is less convincing than it is for segments C1, A and F. However, the possibility that the author did rely upon a text or a formally stable oral form should be kept as an alternative if other evidence (such as that discussed in the follow-up study to this paper) points in that direction.

5.5 STRUCTURE

The identification of any putative structure of *Beowulf* is shaped in great part by variations in plot, setting, subject matter, tone and style. As these same variations can be seen as indicating differences in sources or authorship, all of these questions are tightly intertwined in both this paper and the critical history of the poem. Much of the specific evidence in the preceding section is therefore directly relevant to the discussion here as well. In a sense we have made an artificial division between those theories that view the poem as being composed of many smaller pieces fitted together, which we have discussed above, and those that see it as having a two- or three-part macrostructure, which we discuss in this section.

5.5.1 Two- and Three-Part Structures

As Bjork, Fulk and Niles note, most post-Tolkien analyses of *Beowulf* have divided the poem into either two or three parts.[45] Tolkien himself argued that the structure of the poem mirrors that of the Anglo-Saxon poetic line, with a longer section of the poem, young Beowulf in Denmark, set against the shorter, old Beowulf in Geatland, material. In this view, the two Grendelkin fights in the first section were analogous to the allowable double alliterations in the a-verse of an Anglo-Saxon line, the single dragon fight analogous to required single-alliteration in the b-verse.[46] The majority of critics accept this structural analysis, a division which preceded Tolkien, although the precise location of where to separate the two sections is a matter of some debate, with some critics seeing the break between 1887 and 1888, before Beowulf's retelling of his adventures to Hygelac, and others dividing after line 2199, just before the rapid transition between Beowulf's youth and age.[47] The view that *Beowulf* as we have it is a composite of two pre-existing poems also would place the dividing line around 2199.[48]

Most contemporary proponents of a tripartite structure generally divide *Beowulf* along the lines of the three monster fights: 1–1250 (Grendel), 1251–1888 or 2199 (Grendel's mother), 2200–3182 (the dragon), although there is disagreement about where to place the boundary between the Grendel's mother material and the dragon.[49] However, a different three-part structure was proposed earlier in the critical history of the poem by Levin L. Schücking, who in 1905 argued that the recapitulation material in lines 1888–2199 was a link deliberately forged to join together two originally separate poems. Schücking based his determination on a combination of objective and subjective data, most importantly some syntactic features that he identified as appearing in this passage and nowhere else in *Beowulf*, but also the sense that the recapitulation is tedious and therefore, in a much-repeated logical leap, not to be attributed to the original poet. Schücking's conclusions were rejected as "not proven" by Chambers on the grounds that the concentration of certain constructions in these lines could be "mere accident," that the assertion that the original poet would not have written a tedious passage was arbitrary, and that other uncommon syntactic forms appear not only in the recapitulation but also in the Introduction and the Finn episode, thus undercutting the argument that lines 1888–2199 are syntactically peculiar.[50] Schücking's arguments did not remain influential after Chambers' critique.

We note that the ability of cluster analysis to address questions of the macrostructure of *Beowulf* is confounded by the problem of the change in scribes being nearly coincidental with one of the proposed major divisions of the poem. That the un-normalized dendrogram in Fig. 4.2 places all the material written by the B-Scribe into a single clade cannot by itself be taken as evidence for a two-part division of the poem. As the dendrogram of the normalized text shows, the separation of segments 10–14 from the rest of the text is much more strongly influenced by variations in spelling and orthography than by vocabulary distribution. Furthermore, Fig. 4.2 indicates that segments 2, 3 and 9 are distinctly different than the rest of the poem, a division that is not coincident with any of the proposed two-part structures. The structure suggested by the normalized dendrogram in Fig. 4.9 is somewhat more convincing, since the effects of scribal practice should be eliminated by self-normalization. Here, clade θ divides very neatly around the traditional break-points, with segments B, E, H, I and J clustering together separately from segments K, L, M and N. However, this bimodal divisions excludes a great deal of material: the Unferth episode, the fights with Grendel and his mother, the Proem and the Finnsburg episode, and the very end of the poem. Additionally, in this particular arrangement segment J only contains about half of Beowulf's retelling of his adventures: the rest is found in K. Nevertheless, the dendrogram could be taken as indicating that there is a two-part division in the poem that is not otherwise strongly affected by other factors.

The situation changes only slightly when we consider the fully normalized, hinted and blended text in Fig. 4.10 above. Here again there does seem to be some division between material that comes earlier than segment J and material that comes after. We note that all but one of the segments that are distinctly separated from the large biramous division (C, A and F, and D and G) are from lines 1–1887. That the significant outliers are all from the first half of the poem is not inconsistent with the idea that there is some kind of qualitative division between the first two-thirds and the final third of the poem, although that difference in vocabulary distribution is weak enough to be eclipsed by differences in the vocabulary of those segments that may have different sources. Furthermore, whatever cluster analysis might suggest about a two-part structure for *Beowulf*, the results do not support an identification of a division of the poem along the lines of the three monster fights. The fight with Grendel is consistently similar in vocabulary to the fight with Grendel's mother and is not particularly similar to the dragon fight. We can therefore conclude that, *in terms of vocabulary distribution*,[51] the poem *may* have a two-part structure but does *not* have a three-part structure focused on the monster fights.[52]

5.5.2 Alternate Structures

Although they have not been as influential as the idea that the poem is divided into two movements or three monster-fights, other proposed structures—both three- and four-part—have been proposed for *Beowulf*. In an argument similar to that of Schücking's, Francis P. Magoun suggested that the poem has a tripartite structure, but that the divisions were split not among the monster fights but instead between the events in Denmark, Beowulf's kingship in Geatland, and a bridging or linking passage (lines 1888–2199), composed to join together two originally independent poems, in which Beowulf retells his adventures to Hygelac,[53] Kevin Kiernan's overall analysis is more in the vein of the bipartite structures discussed above, but like Schücking and Magoun he identifies a linking passage within segment J (although his is much shorter than that proposed by the two earlier scholars).[54] Gale Owen-Crocker has argued for seeing *Beowulf* as divided into four sections, each focused around a funeral: Scyld's, Hnaef's, the Last Survivor's, and Beowulf's.[55]

The position of segment J in various dendrograms as well as the separation between pre-J and post-J material would not be inconsistent with the three tripartite analyses. As noted above in §4.4.1, J's placement in a dendrogram varies significantly based on segment boundaries and normalization. J appears to have a relatively weak affinity for the earlier portion of the poem (sometimes linking as an outlier to the clade that contains B, E, H and I), but it can also be made to connect with the material after line 2199. Furthermore, the presence of pieces of J tended to affect the geometry of the dendrograms made in our analysis of the B-Scribe portion of the text, suggesting that there is greater similarity to segments K-Q in the later parts of J than there is in the earlier. These characteristics are also not inconsistent with a hypothesis that the segment has as its source not something outside the poem, but the material from the first part of *Beowulf* itself: the segment would then be an outlier, since it would have a different source than K-Q, but it would also have affinities to the earlier part of the poem, since that was the source of the influence.

This interpretation is similar to Magoun's hypothesis, which was arrived at by an entirely different chain of reasoning focused primarily on supposed discrepancies in the narrative. Schücking, as noted above, was more focused on metrical features and syntactic constructions which were concentrated in what he identified as a bridging passage (segment J) between two originally separate poems. That these elements are also found in the introductory genealogical material (segment A) and the Finn episode (segment F) was used by Chambers to argue against the idea of a bridge between two originally separate poems. But if indeed segments A and F have a different source than the main body of the poem (as the cluster analysis seems to indicate) their inclusion of constructions found otherwise only in J is not necessarily evidence that J is the same as the rest of *Beowulf*. Segment J, however, does not regularly link with the A and F pairing; the three segments may not be similar to each other, only different from the rest of the poem, a conclusion that could support the theory of a three-part *Beowulf* divided among Denmark, Geatland and a bridging passage. Unfortunately, cluster analysis alone cannot resolve the relative priority of A-I, J, or K-Q, nor can it identify specific small-scale features, like those noted by Schücking and Magoun, that would show definitively that it was or was not written separately from the rest of the text.[56] Deleting the lines from J that Kiernan identifies as a shorter bridging passage does not change dendrogram geometry if the segment boundaries are otherwise unshifted, but limits to the resolution of cluster analysis are an impediment to more definitive conclusions.

Owen-Crocker's four-funeral structure is also somewhat consistent with the results of cluster analysis. The funerals in the poem do link together, but in two pairs rather than in a four-part grouping. Scyld's funeral is found in segment A, which is linked to segment F, but this pairing does not link to the pair of K and Q, segments that contain, respectively, the Lay of the Last Survivor and Beowulf's funeral; rather, K and Q link, albeit weakly, to D1 and G1, the Grendelkin fights. Segments A and F link, somewhat more strongly, to L and P, which are made up primarily of Geatish history and the Swedish wars. Nevertheless, the pairing of the funerals is intriguing, and Owen-Crocker's hypothesis deserves additional investigation, especially because we have not identified obvious features of K and Q that would cause these segments to be similar in vocabulary distribution.

It may be that the problem of the macrostructure of *Beowulf* is not entirely amenable to cluster analysis. None of the major proposed structures appears to account for the complete distribution of vocabulary in the poem, particularly the separation of the clades that contain segments C1, D1 and G1, and A and F. The placement of J and the general separation of the A- and B-Scribe portions of the poem could be explained by theories of a composite text welded together somewhere between lines 1888 and 2199, but such an interpretation does not account for the similarities in vocabulary found between the monster fights (D and G) and the pairing of segments K and Q or the albeit weak links between the Danish history material in the first half of the poem (A and F) and the Geatish history in the second (L and P). At this point in our investigation, then, no single proposed macrostructure provides an obvious explanation for the distribution of vocabulary in the entire poem.

5.6 Implications for Authorship Hypotheses

Bjork, Fulk and Niles' fourth edition of Klaeber's *Beowulf* does not even have a heading for "Authorship," indicating not only that contemporary scholars have, generally, given up on this avenue of analysis but also that, "Date, Origins, Influence, Genre" are bound up in any discussion of the characteristics of the author (or authors) of an anonymous poem. Indeed, arguments about the authorship of *Beowulf* are inextricably entwined with arguments about the poem's structure, sources and influences. Lexomic analysis is therefore useful in such analysis only insomuch as it is relevant to these characteristics of *Beowulf*, and so it is not necessary here to rehearse the discussion already given in the sections immediately above.

Nevertheless, it may be useful to note that while cluster analysis does not directly contradict the theory of a single author that so thoroughly dominates contemporary scholarly thought, it does have some implications for any theories that posit multiple authors for the text. Most significantly, the cluster analysis is not entirely consistent with the idea that the fights with Grendel and his mother were written by two separate authors. The linkage of segments D1 and G1 and their separation from the other segments indicates that if they did have two separate authors, the rest of the text would require even more, whose work was even less similar than the authors of the two monster fights in Denmark—a prospect that seems unlikely. Other hypotheses of multiple authorship are not necessarily contraindicated. Each major clade in the poem could have a different author (although this seems unlikely) or there could have been only a single individual who employed multiple discourses. Cluster analysis alone cannot say, but the methods do indicate that there is enough heterogeneity of vocabulary within the text for it to have had a complex textual history that included multiple authors, sources, structures or instantiations.

5.7 Implications for Dating

Cluster analysis measures similarity and difference of vocabulary distribution, so in isolation the method cannot determine the absolute or even the relative priority of any segment of a text. In previous research in Anglo-Saxon poetry, the contents of some outlying segments of a dendrogram were older than the main body of a poem, but in others they were more recent: the Three Youths material appears to antedate the rest of *Daniel*, while *Genesis B* is almost certainly much younger than *Genesis A*. The implications of cluster analysis for the controversial issue of the dating of *Beowulf* therefore require significant interpretation and correlation with other data. From dendrograms alone we cannot conclude that any of the segments C, A and F, and D and G are necessarily older or younger than the rest of the poem or even that all these segments are all in one category or the other. Any one of these groupings could be the core of an older poem around which other material accreted, or a grouping could be material inserted into a later poem, or these segments could be places where the author of *Beowulf* drew upon different sources.

Nevertheless, the heterogeneity of vocabulary distribution detected by cluster analysis has significant implications for other methods of dating the poem. Most importantly, all types of analysis that catalogue or perform general statistical analysis upon the distribution of features in *Beowulf* should take into account the evidence of the dendrogram geometry. For example, as noted in Section 5.5, Chambers rejected Schücking's argument about the distribution of unusual syntactic features because these were not unique to the "bridging" section of the poem but were also found in the introductory genealogical material and the Finnsburg episode. Without necessarily supporting Schücking's larger argument, the dendrogram geometry does provide a plausible explanation for this particular distribution of features: segments A and F could come from a different source, and segment J could have been written by another author. Similar conclusions based on the identification of particular features in both halves or in all three of Shücking's and Magoun's divisions of the poem should be re-examined. Features found only in segments D, G, K and Q or only in A, F, L and P would not necessarily demonstrate a consistency between the Danish and Geatish sections of the poem. Additionally, any single piece of diagnostic information needs to be interpreted in the context of the affinity of its matrix and not be extrapolated without argument to the entire poem. The appearance in a segment of a feature characteristic of a given date range can only be diagnostic for the segment itself and those linked tightly to it, not for the poem as a whole. For instance, if a piece of genealogical information in lines 1–188 suggests a particular date, we are only safe in concluding that segment A and its linked segment F must have been composed before or after that date, not that the entire poem must be.

The methods of rolling window analysis described in the follow-up monograph to the present study provide additional information on the possible antecedents of various segments, which can then be synthesized with both cluster analysis and traditional approaches to shed new light on the textual (and perhaps compositional) history of the poem. For the present it is sufficient to conclude that the heterogeneity of vocabulary indicated by cluster analysis, and the link that has been identified in other Anglo-Saxon poems between that variability and textual sourcing, structure, authorship and dating, means that many arguments about *Beowulf* will need to be re-adjudicated.

Notes

1. Though in less detail than the treatment of the same episode in the Finnsburg Fragment.
2. If linked at all to this historical group, the Lay of the Last Survivor and the Father's Lament are only slightly similar to them in vocabulary.
3. Distribution of function words in a text can serve as a proxy for variations at higher levels of the morpho-semantic hierarchy. See Drout, *Tradition and Influence*, 61–67, 103–108.
4. See T. A. Shippey, "Structure and Unity," in Bjork and Niles, *Beowulf Handbook*, 159–168.
5. See, among others, Charles J. Wright, *The Irish Tradition in Old English Literature*. Cambridge: Cambridge University Press, 1993 (on the description of the mere and the *Visio Pauli*); Leonard Neidorf, "Beowulf before *Beowulf*: Anglo-Saxon Anthroponymy and Heroic Legend," *Review of English Studies* 64 (2013): 553–573 (on Beowulf and the Unferth episode).
6. Drout et al., "Of Dendrogrammatology," 326–335; Downey et al. "Books Tell Us," 162–165, 176–181.
7. Drout et al., "Of Dendrogrammatology," 333–336.
8. Rudolf Koegel, *Geschichte der deutschen Litteratur bis zum ausgange des mittelalters*, vol. 1. Strassburg : K.J. Trübner, 1894–1897, 109. This idea was rejected by Chambers, who asserted, following Hermann Möller, that if there had existed a lay of Beowulf and Breca, the name of the former would be found alongside that of the latter in Widsith (Chambers, *Widsith*,

110; Hermann Möller, *Das altenglische Volksepos in der ursprünglichen strophischen Form*. Kiel: Lipsius & Tischer, 1883, 22).
9. R.W. Chambers, *Widsith: A Study in Old English Heroic Legend*. Cambridge: Cambridge University Press, 1912, 110–111.
10. L.D. Benson, "The Originality of *Beowulf*," in *The Interpretation of Narrative: Theory and Practice*, ed. M.W. Bloomfield (Cambridge, MA, 1970), 1–43; Alistair Campbell, "The Use of *Beowulf* in Earlier Heroic Verse," in *England Before the Conquest*, ed. Peter Clemoes and K. Hughes. Cambridge: Cambridge University Press, 1971, 283–292.
11. Benson, 20–21.
12. Campbell, 284.
13. C.J. Clover, "The Germanic Context of the Unferþ Episode," *Speculum* 55 (1980): 444–468.
14. Fulk, Bjork and Niles, 148–149, 152.
15. Such an interpretation would be consistent with Neidorf, "Beowulf before *Beowulf*," 553–573.
16. An unease based, it seems likely, on fear of becoming one of the "dissectors"—bogeymen who still haunt the rhetoric of contemporary scholarship (cf. Fulk, Bjork and Niles, 278 n.7 and lxxxiv–lxxxvi).
17. Fulk, Bjork and Niles, 278.
18. Alistair Campbell, "The Old English Epic Style," in *English and Medieval Studies presented to J.R.R. Tolkien on the occasion of his seventieth birthday*, ed. Norman Davis and C. Wrenn. London: Allen and Unwin, 1962, 13–26.
19. Fulk, Bjork and Niles, lxxxvi.
20. Fulk, Bjork and Niles, 279.
21. Drout, *Tradition and Influence*, 103–107.
22. "... mit dem Gedichte selbst in keinem nothwendigen Zusammenhange steht," trans. Shippey and Haarder, 231–32. Ludwig Ettmüller, *Beowulf: Heldengedicht des achten Jahrhunderts, zum ersten Male aus dem Angelsächsischen in das Neuhochdeutsche stabreimend übersetzt und mit Einleitung and Anmerkunger versehen*. Zurich: Meyer und Zeller, 1840, 4.
23. Ettmüller, 4, 16–17; trans. Shippey and Haarder, 232–233.
24. Fulk, Bjork and Niles, xlviii–xli, 113.
25. Trans. Shippey and Haarder, 348. Karl Müllenhoff, "Die Innere Geschichte des Beovulfs," *Zeitschrift für deutsches Altertum* 7 (1869): 193–244; reprinted in idem, *Deutsche Altertumskunde*, 5 vols. Berlin: Weidmannsche Buchhandlung, 1870–1900.
26. Fulk, Bjork and Niles, 110. Lines 175–188 are widely regarded as differing in both tone and content from the rest of the poem; Fulk, Bjork and Niles, 127–128. The problem was most famously discussed in the appendix of J.R.R. Tolkien, "*Beowulf*: The Monsters and the Critics," *Proceedings of the British Academy* 22 (1937): 245–295; repr. in *The Monsters and the Critics and Other Essays*, ed. Christopher Tolkien. London: HarperCollins, 1997, 5–48 at 42–44.

27. J.R.R. Tolkien, *Beowulf: A Translation and Commentary Together with Sellic Spell*, ed. Christopher Tolkien. Boston: Houghton Mifflin, 2014, 162–163, our emphasis.
28. Tolkien, *Beowulf: A Translation*, 162, Tolkien's emphasis.
29. Tolkien, *Beowulf: A Translation*, 153.
30. Although it is certainly possible that a rigorous argument for Tolkien's contention may exist somewhere in his voluminous unpublished writings on *Beowulf*.
31. Alcuin, Epistola 81, in *Monumenta Alcuiniana*, ed., P. Jaffé, Bibliotheca Rerum Germanicarum 6. Berlin: Weidmann, 1873, 357; Chambers *Widsith*, 79.
32. Klaeber 4, 110.
33. Personal communication, January 2013.
34. The scholarship on this topic is enormous and far beyond the scope of this paper. For a survey, see Theodore Andersson "Sources and Analogues," in Robert E. Bjork and John D. Niles, *A Beowulf Handbook*, 125–148.
35. Alois Brandl, "Zur Entstehung der germanischen Heldensage, gesehen vom angelsächsischen Standpunkt," *Archiv für das Studium der neueren Sprachen und Literaturen* 162 (1932): 191–202 at 193, trans. Theodore M. Andersson in Bjork and Niles, *Beowulf Handbook*, 134.
36. Andersson, 129–134, 146–148. The Bear's Son Tale was first identified as a parallel by Friedrich Panzer, *Studien zur germanischen Sagengeschichte, I: Beowulf*. Munich: Beck, 1910. For the most detailed and convincing discussion see Peter A. Jorgensen, "The Two-Troll Variant of the Bear's Son Folktale in *Hálfdanar saga Brönufóstra* and *Gríms saga loðinkinna*," *Arv: Journal of Scandinavian Folklore* 31 (1975): 35–43 and idem "Additional Icelandic Analogues to *Beowulf*," in *Sagnaskemmetun: Studies in Honour of Hermann Pálsson on his 65th Birthday, 26 May, 1986*, ed. Rudolf Simek, Jónas Kristjánsson and Hans Bekker-Nielsen. Vienna: Hermann Böhlaus Nachfolger, 201–208.
37. Andersson 144–145; Fulk, Bjork and Niles, xci.
38. Ironically, Tolkien himself thought that the poet had, at the very least, a specific and detailed folktale source. See below and Tolkien, *Beowulf: A Translation*, 355–414.
39. Tolkien's lecture is in part an argument *contra* Ker; see J.R.R. Tolkien, *Beowulf and the Critics*, rev. 2nd ed., ed. Michael D.C. Drout. Tempe: Arizona Medieval and Renaissance Texts and Studies, 2011 [2003], xxiii–xxv, 6–7.
40. Magnús Fjalldal, *The Long Arm of Coincidence: The Frustrated Connection Between Beowulf and Grettis Saga*. Toronto: University of Toronto Press, 1998.

41. Larry D. Benson, "The Originality of *Beowulf*," Anatoly Liberman, "Beowulf—Grettir," in *Germanic Dialects: Linguistic and Philological Investigations*, ed. Bela Brogyanyi and Thomas Krömmelbein. Amsterdam: J. Benjamins, 1986, 353–401.
42. Tolkien, *Beowulf: A Translation*, 360–403. Tolkien also translates part of his tale into Old English prose.
43. John Leyerle, "The Interlace Structure of *Beowulf*," *University of Toronto Quarterly* 37 (1961): 1–17.
44. Or, for that matter, material from two or more sources.
45. Fulk, Bjork and Niles, lxxix–lxxxi.
46. Tolkien, "*Beowulf*: The Monsters and the Critics," 29–32; "Tolkien's explication of the poem's larger structure, though frequently disputed has never been bettered, and the methodology inherent in his practice of basing claims about the macrostructural level on patterns everyone discerns in the microstructure remains a model for emulation," R. D. Fulk, "Preface," in *Interpretations of Beowulf*, ed. R.D. Fulk, Bloomington: Indiana University Press, 1991, ix–xix at xi.
47. For instance, Charles Donahue sees the end of Part 1 as the passage on Hrothgar's death (1885–1887) ("Beowulf and Christian Tradition: A Reconsideration from a Celtic Stance," *Traditio* 21 [1965]: 55–116 at p. 86); for a similar view see Bernard F. Huppé, *The Hero in the Earthly City: A Reading of Beowulf* Binghamton. State University of New York Press, 1984, 69. However, most critics favor 2199 as the break in a two-part structure. See for example Tolkien, "*Beowulf*: The Monsters and the Critics," 29; W. P. Ker, *Epic and Romance* 1897; rpt. New York: Macmillan, 1957, p. 161; Frederick Klaeber, *Beowulf and the Fight at Finnsburg*. Boston: D. C. Heath, 1922, xi; Robert E. Kaske, "Sapientia et Fortitudo as the Controlling Theme of Beowulf," *Studies in Philology* 55, no. 3 (July 1958): 423–457 at 427; Arthur G. Brodeur, *The Art of Beowulf*. Berkeley: University of California Press, 1959), p. 72; and Edward B. Irving, Jr., *A Reading of Beowulf*. New Haven: Yale University Press, 1968, 192. Tolkien himself seems to have changed his mind on this score; in his recently published translation of *Beowulf* he locates the division after line 1887, stating in the commentary to line 1887: "Here ends the 'First Part' of Beowulf." The commentary goes on to refer to lines 1888–2199 as "the Link or Interlude" (*Beowulf: A Translation*, 312) whereas in "The Monsters and the Critics" he is unequivocal that the first part ends at line 2199: "A from 1 to 2199 (including an exordium of 52 lines); B from 2200 to 3182 (the end)."
48. Kevin Kiernan, *Beowulf and the Beowulf Manuscript*. Ann Arbor: University of Michigan Press, 1981, 251–278.
49. Fulk, Bjork and Niles, lxxix–lxxxi.

50. R. W. Chambers, *Beowulf: An Introduction to the Study of the Poem with a Discussion of the Stories of Offa and Finn*, suppl. by C. L. Wrenn. Cambridge: Cambridge University Press, 1963, 117–120.
51. We draw no conclusions about the structure in terms of theme, character development, political allegory or other structuring principles at a level of abstraction above that of vocabulary distribution.
52. The proposals for a tripartite structure are far too numerous to list here; see Fulk, Bjork and Niles, lxxx notes 3, 4, and 5 for an extensive list. See also the discussion by Shippey in Bjork and Niles, *Beowulf Handbook*, 164–168 and Katherine Hume, "The Theme and Structure of *Beowulf*," *Studies in Philology* 72, no. 1 (January 1975): 1–27 at 3, note 5.
53. Schücking 1905; Francis Peabody Magoun, "Beowulf A': A Folk Variant," *Arv: Journal of Scandinavian Folklore* 14 (1958): 95–101 and "Beowulf B: A Folk-Tale of Beowulf's Death," in *Early English and Norse Studies Presented to Hugh Smith in Honour of His Sixtieth Birthday*, London: Methuen, 1963, 127–140.
54. Kiernan argues that folio 179r is a palimpsest and that therefore the lines around 2199 are where the B-Scribe re-worked the manuscript to forge an improved transition between two poems he had brought together. Kevin Kiernan, *Beowulf and the Beowulf Manuscript*. Ann Arbor: University of Michigan Press, 1996 (1981): 219–242.
55. Gale Owen-Crocker, *The Four Funerals in Beowulf: And the Structure of the Poem*. Manchester: Manchester University Press, 2000.
56. The methods in Part 2 may, however, shed additional light on the problem, since they can be used to track the presence or absence of features much smaller than the 700–1000-word resolution limit.

CHAPTER 6

Conclusions Drawn from Cluster Analysis

Abstract Cluster analysis indicates the presence of different discourses within *Beowulf*. Segments C (Breca/Unferth), A (Proem) and F (Finnsburg) are very likely to have been influenced by sources different from those of the majority of the poem. Segments D (Grendel Fight), G (Grendel's mother), L (Geatish history) and P (Geatish/Swedish Wars) are also likely to have been influenced by sources, with the sources of L and P being like (or even the same as) those of A and F. Segment J (bridge or recapitulation) may have a source as well, although that source may be the earlier part of *Beowulf* itself. Smaller sub-sections of the poem—among them, the Offa and Thryth digression and the story of Freawaru and the Heathobards—appear to have at least weak affinity with the robust pairing of A and F. The particularly strong effects of "Joy in the Hall" (lines 607–661), "The Father's Lament" (2444–2462a), "The Lay of the Last Survivor" (2247–2270b), and Wiglaf's criticism of the cowardly retainers (2860–2891) on dendrogram geometries suggest that there is something unusual about these segments. Material in lines 1–1887 tends to cluster together, as does that of lines 2200–3182, but there are connections and links across those broad divisions.

Keywords *Beowulf* • Cluster analysis • Lexomics • Sources • *Beowulf*, author of • *Beowulf*, sources of • *Beowulf*, scribes of • "Lay of the Last Survivor" • "Father's Lament" • Freawaru • Finnsburg • Geats • Swedes • Danes • Legendary history • Dendrogram

When applied to the text of *Beowulf*, methods of cluster analysis produce results that are neither trivial nor bizarre but instead appear to be consistent with analyses of the poem based on entirely different approaches. Although cluster analysis is limited in resolution (due to minimum segment size) and dependent upon the placement of segment boundaries, both problems can, to some degree, be addressed by the production and analysis of many dendrograms with varying segment sizes and boundaries. Use of a self-normalized text of *Beowulf* allows us to eliminate patterns based solely on scribal practice and instead focus on those of word distribution. The robust results of such analyses indicate that vocabulary distribution is heterogeneous and that there are patterns of similarity among various segments that are not entirely independent of the content of those segments.

Our conclusions:

(a) Cluster analysis indicates the presence of different discourses within *Beowulf*.[1]

(b) Segments C, A and F are very likely to have been influenced by sources different from those (if any) of the majority of the poem.

(c) Segments D, G, L and P are also likely to have been influenced by sources, with the sources of L and P being like (or even the same as) those of A and F.

(d) Segment J's behavior in various dendrograms is unusual enough for us not to reject the notion that it may have a source as well, although that source may be the earlier part of *Beowulf* itself.

(e) Smaller sub-sections of the poem—among them, the Offa and Thryth digression and the story of Freawaru and the Heathobards—appear to have at least weak affinity with the robust pairing of A and F, but these segments are generally too short for us to be certain of the relationships.

(f) The particularly strong effects of "Joy in the Hall" (lines 607–661), "The Father's Lament" (2444–2462a), "The Lay of the Last Survivor" (2247–2270b), and Wiglaf's criticism of the cowardly retainers (2860–2891) on dendrogram geometries suggest that there is something unusual about these segments. Cluster analysis alone, however, can not determine the cause of these effects.

(g) The material in lines 1–1887 tends to cluster together, as does that of lines 2200–3182, but there are connections and links across those broad divisions. All of the major outlying clades contain material from the first part of the poem, and segment J has more affinity for this earlier material than for the latter. Determining whether or not these tendencies are indicative of the macrostructure or the authorship of the poem remains beyond the capabilities of cluster analysis alone, although we can say that a three-part structure organized solely around the monster fights is inconsistent with the evidence of cluster analysis.

Some of these conclusions will be further supported—and some will be complicated—by the results of rolling window analysis,[2] which produce additional and somewhat independent evidence that can be used for the detection of segment boundaries, and which may allow us to determine whether some of the putative sources for various segments were oral or written, Latin or Old English. But for the present, it is sufficient to conclude that methods of cluster analysis have extracted new and unexpected information from the text of *Beowulf*, the most significant of which is that the poem almost certainly had multiple sources that were distinct in form, not merely in the sense that the poet was generally aware of traditions or other stories. This information allows us—indeed it requires us—to reopen questions about the poem that have long been thought to be unanswerable. This is a project both difficult and not necessarily wished for by contemporary scholarship, but the reward is a significantly improved understanding of *Beowulf* and the culture in which it was created.

Notes

1. This heterogeneity of the poem has significant implications for types of analysis that reach conclusions based on the frequency and distribution in the poem of specific orthographic, morphological, syntactic or metrical features. As will be discussed in detail in the follow-up to this study, the distribution of particular features is correlated with (but not the cause of) the overall distribution of vocabulary in the poem. Localization of features to specific sections must be taken into account when analyzing the poem. For example, a feature that appears only in segments A and F, cannot necessarily be used to draw conclusion about the rest of *Beowulf*.
2. Described in the follow-up to this study, *Beowulf Unlocked II: Rolling Window Analysis*.

BIBLIOGRAPHY

Alcuin. 1873. "Epistola 81." In *Monumenta Alcuiniana*, edited by P. Jaffé, Bibliotheca Rerum Germanicarum 6. Berlin: Weidmann.

Andersson, Theodore. 1998. "Sources and Analogues." In *A Beowulf Handbook*, edited by Robert E. Bjork and John D. Niles, 125–148. Lincoln, NE: University of Nebraska Press.

Benson, L. D. 1970. "The Originality of *Beowulf*." In *The Interpretation of Narrative: Theory and Practice*, edited by M. W. Bloomfield, 1–43. Cambridge, MA: Harvard University Press.

Berger, Rosetta, and Michael D. C. Drout. 2015. "A Reconsideration of the Relationship Between *Víga-Glúms Saga* and *Reykdæla Saga*: New Evidence from Lexomic Analysis." *Viking and Medieval Scandinavia*, 11 (2015): 1–32.

Boyd, Phoebe, Michael D. C. Drout, Namiko Hitotsubashi, Michael J. Kahn, Mark D. LeBlanc, and Leah Smith. 2014. "Lexomic Analysis of Anglo-Saxon Prose: Establishing Controls with the Old English Penitential and the Old English Translation of Orosius." *Revista de la Sociedad Española de Lengua y Literatura Inglesa Medieval (SELIM)* 19: 7–58.

Brandl, Alois. 1932. "Zur Entstehung der germanischen Heldensage, gesehen vom angelsächsischen Standpunkt." *Archiv für das Studium der neueren Sprachen und Literaturen* 162: 191–202.

Brodeur, Arthur G. 1959. *The Art of Beowulf*. Berkeley: University of California Press.

Brunetti, Giuseppe. Accessed November 2014. http://www.maldura.unipd.it/dllags/brunetti/OE/TESTI/Beowulf/index.htm

Burrows, John F. 2002. "The Englishing of Juvenal: Computational Stylistics and Translated Texts." *Style* 36 (4): 677–699.

Burrows, John F. 2003. "Questions of Authorship: Attribution and Beyond." *Computers and the Humanities* 37: 5–32.
Campbell, Alistair. 1962. "The Old English Epic Style." In *English and Medieval Studies Presented to J.R.R. Tolkien on the Occasion of his Seventieth Birthday*, edited by Norman Davis and C. L. Wrenn, 13–26. London: Allen and Unwin.
Campbell, Alistair. 1971. "The Use of *Beowulf* in Earlier Heroic Verse." In *England Before the Conquest*, edited by Peter Clemoes and K. Hughes, 283–292. Cambridge: Cambridge University Press.
Chambers, R.W. 1912. *Widsith: A Study in Old English Heroic Legend*. Cambridge: Cambridge University Press.
Chambers, R. W. 1963. *Beowulf: An Introduction to the Study of the Poem with a Discussion of the Stories of Offa and Finn*, suppl. by C. L. Wrenn. Cambridge: Cambridge University Press.
Clover, C. J. 1980. "The Germanic Context of the Unferþ Episode." *Speculum* 55: 444–468.
Dobbie, Elliott Van Kirk, ed. 1953. *Beowulf and Judith*. New York: Columbia University Press.
Donahue, Charles. 1965. "Beowulf and Christian Tradition: A Reconsideration from a Celtic Stance." *Traditio* 21: 55–116.
Downey, Sarah, Michael D. C. Drout, Michael J. Kahn, and Mark D. LeBlanc. 2012. "'Books Tell Us': Lexomic and Traditional Evidence for the Sources of *Guthlac A*." *Modern Philology* 110: 1–29.
Downey, Sarah, Michael D. C. Drout, Veronica Kerekes, and Douglas Raffle. 2014. "Lexomic Analysis of Medieval Latin Texts." *Journal of Medieval Latin* 24: 225–274.
Drout, Michael D. C., and Elie Chauvet. 2015. "Tracking the Moving Ratio of *þ* to *ð* in Anglo-Saxon Texts: A New Method, and Evidence for a Lost Old English Version of the 'Song of the Three Youths.'" *Anglia* 133 (2): 278–319.
Drout, Michael D. C., Namiko Hitotsubashi, and Rachel Scavera. 2014. "Tolkien's Creation of the Impression of Depth." *Tolkien Studies* 11: 167–211.
Drout, Michael D. C., Michael J. Kahn, Mark D. LeBlanc, and Christina Nelson. 2011. "Of Dendrogrammatology: Lexomic Methods for Analyzing the Relationships Among Old English Poems." *Journal of English and Germanic Philology* 110: 301–336.
Drout, Michael D. C., Elizabeth Peterson, Ann Marie Brasacchio, and Yun Meng. "Lexomic Analysis of Shakespeare's Collaborations." [forthcoming].
Drout, Michael D. C., and Leah Smith. "A Pebble in the Stream of Tradition: 'Joy in the Hall,' (Lines 607–661 in *Beowulf*)." [forthcoming].
Dyer, Betsey Dexter. 2002. "Blunt End." *Genome Technology* 1.27. Accessed November 2014. http://www.genomeweb.com/blunt-end-0

Ettmüller, Ludwig. 1840. *Beowulf: Heldengedicht des achten Jahrhunderts, zum ersten Male aus dem Angelsächsischen in das Neuhochdeutsche stabreimend übersetzt und mit Einleitung and Anmerkunger versehen*. Zurich: Meyer und Zeller.
Fjalldal, Magnús. 1998. *The Long Arm of Coincidence: The Frustrated Connection Between Beowulf and Grettis Saga*. Toronto: University of Toronto Press.
Frantzen, Allen J. 1990. *Desire for Origins: New Language, Old English and Teaching the Tradition*. New Brunswick: Rutgers University Press.
Fulk, R. D. 1991. "Preface." In *Interpretations of Beowulf*, edited by R. D. Fulk, ix–xix. Bloomington: Indiana University Press.
Fulk, R. D. 1997. "Textual Criticism." In *A Beowulf Handbook*, edited by Robert E. Bjork and John D. Niles, 35–53. Lincoln: University of Nebraska Press.
Fulk, R.D., Robert E. Bjork, and John D. Niles. 2008. *Klaeber's Beowulf, Fourth Edition*. Toronto: University of Toronto Press.
Gerritsen, Johan. 1989. "Have with You to Lexington! The *Beowulf* Manuscript and *Beowulf*." In *In Other Words, Transcultural Studies in Philology, Translation and Lexicography Presented to Hans Heinrich Meier on the Occasion of his Sixty-Fifth Birthday*, edited by J. Mackenzie and R. Todd, 15–34. Dordrecht: Foris.
Hoover, David L. 2004. "Testing Burrows's Delta." *Literary and Linguistic Computing* 19 (4): 453–475.
Hume, Katherine. 1975. "The Theme and Structure of *Beowulf*." *Studies in Philology* 72 (1): 1–27.
Huppé, Bernard F. 1984. *The Hero in the Earthly City: A Reading of Beowulf*. Binghamton: State University of New York Press.
Irving Jr., Edward B. 1968. *A Reading of Beowulf*. New Haven: Yale University Press.
Jorgensen, Peter A. 1975. "The Two-Troll Variant of the Bear's Son Folktale in *Hálfdanar saga Brönufóstra* and *Gríms saga loðinkinna*." *Arv: Journal of Scandinavian Folklore* 31: 35–43.
Jorgensen, Peter A. 1986. "Additional Icelandic Analogues to *Beowulf*." In *Sagnaskemmtun: Studies in Honour of Hermann Pálsson on his 65th Birthday, 26 May, 1986*, edited by Rudolf Simek, Jónas Kristjánsson, and Hans Bekker-Nielsen, 201–208. Vienna: Hermann Böhlaus Nachfolger.
Kaske, Robert E. 1958. "Sapientia et Fortitudo as the Controlling Theme of *Beowulf*." *Studies in Philology* 55 (3): 423–457.
Ker, W. P. 1957 [1897] *Epic and Romance*. New York: Macmillan.
Kiernan, Kevin. 1996 [1981]. *Beowulf and the Beowulf Manuscript*. Ann Arbor: University of Michigan Press.
Kiernan, Kevin, ed. 1999. *The Electronic Beowulf*. London: British Library.
Kisor, Yvette. 2009. "Numerical Composition and *Beowulf*: A Reconsideration." *Anglo-Saxon England* 38: 41–76.
Klaeber, Fr. 1922. *Beowulf and the Fight at Finnsburg*. Boston: D. C. Heath.

Koegel, Rudolf. 1894–1897. *Geschichte der deutschen Litteratur bis zum ausgange des mittelalters*, vol. 1. Strassburg: K. J. Trübner.
Leerssen, Joep. 2006. *National Thought in Europe: A Cultural History*. Amsterdam: Amsterdam University Press.
Leyerle, John. 1961. "The Interlace Structure of *Beowulf*." *University of Toronto Quarterly* 37: 1–17.
Liberman, Anatoly. 1986. "Beowulf—Grettir." In *Germanic Dialects: Linguistic and Philological Investigations*, edited by Bela Brogyanyi and Thomas Krömmelbein, 353–401. Amsterdam: J. Benjamins.
Magoun, Francis Peabody, Jr., ed. 1958. "Beowulf A': A Folk Variant." *Arv: Journal of Scandinavian Folklore* 14: 95–101.
Magoun, Francis Peabody, Jr., ed. 1963. "Beowulf B: A Folk-Tale of Beowulf's Death." In *Early English and Norse Studies Presented to Hugh Smith in Honour of His Sixtieth Birthday*, edited by Arthur Brown and Peter Foote, 127–140. London: Methuen.
Magoun, Francis Peabody, Jr., ed. 1965 [1956]. *The Anglo-Saxon Poems in Bright's Anglo-Saxon Reader Done in Normalized Orthography*. Cambridge, MA: Harvard University Press.
Magoun, Francis Peabody, Jr., ed. 1966 [1959]. *Béowulf and Judith Done in a Normalized Orthography*, Rev. 2nd ed., edited by Jess B. Bessinger, Jr. Cambridge: Harvard University Press.
Möller, Hermann. 1883. *Das altenglische Volksepos in der ursprünglichen strophischen Form*. Kiel: Lipsius & Tischer.
Moretti, Franco. 2005. *Graphs, Maps and Trees: Abstract Models for a Literary History*. London: Verso.
Müllenhoff, Karl. 1869. "Die Innere Geschichte des Beovulfs." *Zeitschrift für deutsches Altertum* 7: 193–244; Reprinted in idem, *Deutsche Altertumskunde*, 5 vols. Berlin: Weidmannsche Buchhandlung, 1870–1900.
Neidorf, Leonard. 2013. "Beowulf before *Beowulf*: Anglo-Saxon Anthroponymy and Heroic Legend." *Review of English Studies* 64: 553–573.
Owen-Crocker, Gale. 2000. *The Four Funerals in Beowulf: And the Structure of the Poem*. Manchester: Manchester University Press.
Panzer, Friedrich. 1910. *Studien zur germanischen Sagengeschichte, I: Beowulf*. Munich: Beck.
Schücking, Levin. 1905. *Beowulfs Rückkehr: eine kritische Studie*. Studien zur englischen Philologie 21. Halle: Max Niemeyer.
Shippey, T. A. 1998. "Structure and Unity." In *A Beowulf Handbook*, edited by Robert E. Bjork and John D. Niles, 159–168. Lincoln, NE: University of Nebraska Press.
Shippey, T.A. 2005. *The Shadow-Walkers: Jacob Grimm's Mythology of the Monstrous*. Tempe: Arizona Center for Medieval and Renaissance Texts and Studies.

Shippey, T.A., and Andreas Haarder. 1998. *Beowulf: The Critical Heritage*. London: Routledge.
Tolkien, J.R.R. 1937. "*Beowulf:* The Monsters and the Critics." *Proceedings of the British Academy* 22: 245–295; Reprinted in J.R.R. Tolkien. 1997. *The Monsters and the Critics and Other Essays*, edited by Christopher Tolkien, 5–48. London: HarperCollins.
Tolkien, J.R.R. 2011 [2003]. *Beowulf and the Critics*, Rev. 2nd ed., edited by Michael D. C. Drout. Tempe: Arizona Medieval and Renaissance Texts and Studies.
Tolkien, J.R.R. 2014. *Beowulf: A Translation and Commentary Together with Sellic Spell*. Edited by Christopher Tolkien. Boston: Houghton Mifflin.
Wawn, Andrew, Graham Johnson, and John Walter. 2007. *Constructing Nations, Reconstructing Myth: Essay in Honour of T. A. Shippey*. Turnhout: Brepols.
Wright, Charles J. 1993. *The Irish Tradition in Old English Literature*. Cambridge: Cambridge University Press.
Zupitza, Julius, ed. 1959. *Beowulf: Reproduced in Facsimile from the Unique Manuscripts British Museum MS. Cotton Vitellius A.xv*. 2nd ed. Oxford: Early English Text Society.

Index

A
Alcuin, 65
Andersson, Theodore, 4, 78
Anglo-Saxon Poetic Records editions of poems, 18
arrivals and departures, representations of, 51
artifacts, produced by segment division, 11
Æschere, 28
attacks
 on Heorot by Grendel, 31
 on Heorot by Grendel's mother, 69
Azarias, 6, 10, 21, 24 (see also *Daniel*, *Song of the Three Youths*)

B
"Bear's Son Tale," 66, 67, 68
Benson, Larry D., 62, 69, 80
beot, 39, 40, 48, 59
Beow, 64
Beowulf and Judith, ed. Dobbie, 18
Beowulf, authorship of, 75
Beowulf, composite nature of, 75
Beowulf, composition of, 70
Beowulf, critical editions of, 21
Beowulf, critical history of, 70
Beowulf, dating of, 76
Beowulf, divisions of
 at line 2209a, 49
 between lines 1888–2199, 71
 between lines 1888–3182, 42
 between lines 1887 and 1888, 33, 49, 71
 scribal division at 1939b, 36
Beowulf, facsimile of, 21
Beowulf, features of
 implications of distribution for dating, 76
Beowulf, lines of
 1–52, 65
 1–1887, 42
 175–188, 65
 2209a, 49
 1939b–3182, 36
Beowulf, proem, 34, 46, 50, 58, 64–67, 76 (see also "*Beowulf*, lines 1-52"; "Danish History"; "Scyld Scefing)

Beowulf, scribes of, 19
  A-Scribe, 19
  B-Scribe, 19, 72–73
Beowulf, segments of (see also "segments")
Beowulf, structure of, 26, 70, 74
  alternate structures, 73
  three-part, 71, 73; based on monster fights, 71
  two-part, 71
bioinformatics, 5
Bjork, Robert E., 19, 38, 62
blending, technique of, 30, 31, 49, 69
  and deleting, 49
boundaries of segments, 12 (see also "segments")
Brandl, Alois, 67
Breca, 30, 33, 34, 58, 59 (see also Unferth)
bridging passages, 74
  arrangement of segments within, 36
Brisinga mene, 53
Brunetti, Giuseppe, 20
Burrows, John F., 5, 14

C

Caesarius of Arles, 16
Campbell, Alistair, 62–63
Chambers, R.W., 71, 74, 76, 77
chiasmus, 59
Christ I, II, III, 6
Christ III, 16, 67
clades, 8–10
  correlation with sources, 61
  identifying boundaries of, 10–12
clade structure
  interpretation of, 8, 24
Clover, Carol, 62
cluster analysis, 2, 7–9, 61, 83
  interpretation of, 56
clustering methods, 7–9
  weaknesses of, 3

color metaphor, 11
consolidation, technique of, 18
corpus linguistics, 5
Cotton fire, damage to manuscript caused by, 18
"creation hymn" in *Beowulf*, 65
Cynewulf, 6, 10, 24

D

Dæghrefn, 39, 40
Damico, Helen, 67
Danes, historical background of, 28, 30, 63, 66 (see also "proem")
Daniel, 6, 10, 21, 24, 64, 67, 76 (see also, *Azarias, Song of the Three Youths*)
deletion, technique of
  incremental, 36
dendrograms, 9
  of A-Scribe material, 34
  of B-Scribe material, 36–39
  as dynamical system, 12
  geometries of, 9; correlation with sources, 14; interpretation of, 24, 26
  robust geometries of, 24
  screening, 1200-word segments, 24
  stepwise geometry of, 10
Denmark, 27, 30, 48, 49, 53, 59–60, 68, 70, 71, 73–75
Dictionary of Old English corpus, 18
diphthongs
  spelling of, 19
discourses, 59–61
  "battle," 59–60
  "hall," 58–59
  "historical," 58–60
  interwoven, 51, 58–60
  "journey," 59, 60
  "monster treasure," 58–59, 60
  patterns of, 61
  "recapitulation," 57–60

"Unferth," 58–59
"dissectors," 63
  fear of being one, 78
"distant reading," 6
Dobbie, Elliott van Kirk, 18
Doom of the Geats, 40, 49
dragon, 70
  attack by, 51
  episodic nature of fight against, 35
  fight against, 27, 53, 58
  fight against by Beowulf and Wiglaf, 40, 58
  killing of by Beowulf, 40
  segments in which fighting occurs, 50–51
"dragon blend" blending, 39
Dyer, Betsey Dexter, 3

E
editions of *Beowulf*
  critical, 19; *KL4*, 19; *Klaeber's Beowulf and the Fight at Finnsburg*, 19
  diplomatic, 21
  lemmatized, 20; Brunetti, 20
  normalized, 19–21; Magoun, 19–20; NormKL4, 20
envelope pattern, 27, 40, 60
eorðbuend, 64
eorðcyning, 64
epiphenomena, 61
episcopus (abbreviation for), 21
eth <ð>, 17
Ettmüller, Ludwig, 64
Euclidean distance, 15
Exeter Book, 6, 21

F
"Fall of the Angels," 67
"Father's Lament," 38, 40, 49–51, 53, 60, 77

fights
  against the dragon, 27, 40, 58
  against the Grendelkin, 51, 58, 67–69
Finnsburg episode, 27–28, 32, 48, 53, 58, 63–66, 69, 76
Finnsburg fragment, 62–64
Fitts, 20–23
Fjalldal, Magnús, 79
flyting, 63
folktale, 68
Freawaru, 49, 50–53, 58, 60, 83
Fulk, R. D., 19, 38, 62
funeral(s)
  Beowulf's, 40, 51, 58, 60, 74
  and buried treasure, 39, 40
  four funeral hypothesis, 73–74 (see also "Owen-Crocker, Gayle")

G
Geatland, return to, 33
Geats
  history of, 27, 39–40, 46, 48, 50, 51, 74
  succession of, 38–40, 50–53
Genesis (Old English), 10
Genesis A, 64, 67, 76
Genesis A and *B*, 6
Genesis B, 76
  "Fall of the Angels," 67
Gerritsen, Johann, 4
gift-giving, 34
Grendel
  attack of, 27, 59
  Beowulf's fight against, 24, 33
Grendelkin material
  sources of, 47, 67
Grendel's mother
  attack of, 27, 59
  Beowulf's fight against, 30–31, 53
Grettis saga, 67–69
Guthlac A, 10, 64 (see also "hellmouth")
Guthlac A and B, 6, 24
Guthlac B, 6, 10

H

Haarder, Andreas, 3
Halga, 65
"hall business," 51, 59
"hall discourse," 59–60
"hall" grouping, 58
"Hand and the Child," 67
Hathcyn, death of, 39
Heathobards, 49, 50, 58, 66, 83
hellmouth
 episode in *Guthlac*, 67
Heremod, 54, 59
hildeleoma, 64
hinting, technique of, 12, 28–30
historical discourse, 59–60
 historical and political material, 53
"historical" group, 58
homogeneity, 11
 of B-Scribe text, 36
Hoover, David L., 5, 14
Hrethel, death of, 38
Hrólfssaga kraka, 67
Hrothgar, 27, 59
 daughter of, 65
 reading of sword hilt by, 60
 sermon by, 53
Hygelac, 27
Hygelac and Heardred, deaths of, 38–39, 49

I

incrementation, technique of, 13
Ingeld, 66
interlacement, 69

J

"journey" discourse, 59–60
journey to the mere, 59–60
"Joy in the Hall," 31, 40, 54, 59, 83
Juliana, 64

K

Ker, W. P., 66, 68
Kiernan, Kevin, 21, 73–74, 80
KL4, 19
Klaeber's Beowulf and the Fight at Finnsburg, 19
Koegel, Rudolf, 62

L

LaBrie, Courtney, 53
Latin
 lexomic analysis of, 6
"Lay of the Last Survivor," 38, 49–53, 58, 74, 77
Leerssen, Joep, 3
lemmatization, 18
lexomic methods, 2
 definition of, 5
Leyerle, John, 80
Liberman, Anatoly, 69
Liedertheorie, 64

M

Magoun, Francis P., 19, 22, 73–74
mark-up
 removal of, 17
merged segments
 artificial homogeneity of, 48
Middle English
 lexomic analysis of, 6
Modern English
 lexomic analysis of, 6
Möller, Hermann, 77
"monster and treasure" group, 58
monsters
 combats against, 30, 43, 51, 68
 defining *Beowulf*, 68
"monster treasure" discourse, 58–59, 60
Moretti, Franco, 6
morpho-semantic hierarchy, 77
Müllenhoff, Karl, 64–66

N
Neidorf, Leonard, 77
Niles, John D., 19, 38, 62
normalization, 20
normalized text, 36
  Normed KL4, 20, 44–47

O
Offa, 50
Old English Penitential, 6, 10, 14
Old Norse
  lexomic analysis of, 6
Ongentheow, 40
Orosius' *Historiae adversus paganos*, 10
orthographic variation
  consistency of, 19
orthography, 17
  effects on cluster analysis, 19
Owen-Crocker, Gayle, 73–74
  (see also "four funeral hypothesis")

P
Panzer, Friedrich, 68, 78
premature interpretation, 57
proem, 34, 46, 50, 58, 64–67, 76
  (see also "Danish History")
punctuation, 17

R
recapitulation, 27, 57–59, 71
retelling of adventures, 49
  (See also recapitulation)
revenge
  for Hygelac, 40
ribbon diagram, 11, 24, 49, 53, 70
Richardson diagram, 53
robust geometries, 12, 28–30, 48
rolling window analysis, 3

S
sanctus (*abbreviation for*), 21
Schücking, Levin L., 4, 71, 74, 76
scrabble diagram, 34, 35, 51
screening dendrogram, 23–27
  of A-Scribe Text, 27–29
  of B-Scribe Text, 35
scribal variation, 61
scribes, 19
Scriftboc, 10
scrubbing, technique of, 17
Scyld, 27–30, 50, 64, 73–74
segmentation
  A-Scribe Text, 28, 32
  B-Scribe Text, 35
segment boundaries, 10, 23, 32
  identification of, 11
segments
  groupings of, 57;
    B1, E1, H1 and I, 48, 57, 73;
    D1, G1, K1 and Q1, 51, 70;
    E1, H1, B1, I, 48, 50;
    M, N1 and O1, 50, 57, 60
  individual;
    A, source of, 66;
    C, 29;
    C1, 29, 48, 53, 58, 62–63;
    C1: source of, 63;
    E1, 57;
    J, 33, 36, 48–49, 53, 59–60, 72, 73, 74;
    K, 38;
    L, 50;
    M, 40;
    N, 40;
    O, 40;
    O1, 40;
    X, 50;
    Y, 50
  pairings of;
    B1 and I, 57;
    D1 and G1, 34, 47–50, 58, 67–69, 75;

segments (*cont.*)
   A and F, 29, 47–48, 50–53, 66;
   J and K, 48;
   J and K: boundary between, 36;
   K and Q, 38, 40, 47, 48, 50, 58, 60;
   L and P, 39–40, 45–48, 53, 58, 60;
   N and O, 40;
   N1 and O1, 40
  sizes of, 24;
  optimal, 10
Sellic Spell, 69
shifting (technique of), 13, 28, 38
Shippey, T. A., 3, 77
Sievers, Eduard, 6
Sigemund, 27–28, 54, 59
Song of the Three Youths, 6, 14, 67, 76 (see also *Azarias, Daniel*)
sources, 61, 68
  external, 67, 70
stability
  in form, 68, 69
stepwise geometry of dendrograms
  significance of, 34, 47, 58
structure (see also *Beowulf*, structure of)
stylometry, computational, 6
Swedish wars, 38–39, 46, 48–51, 58, 74
swimming exploits, 62 (see also Breca, Unferth)
sword hilt
  reading of by Hrothgar, 60
swurdleoma, 64
synthesis
  of cluster analysis, 51

T

tagging, removal of, 17 (see also "mark-up")
text analysis
  A-Scribe and B-Scribe together, 42
texts
  heterogeneity of, 61
  history of, 75
  preparation of, 17

thorn <þ>, 17, 21
Thryth, 50, 51, 53, 58
Tironian note, 17–18, 21
Tolkien, J.R.R., 61, 65
  "*Beowulf*: The Monsters and the Critics," 68
truncation (technique of), 13
"Two-Troll Tale," 68

U

Unferth, 30, 33–35, 58–59, 77
  segment, 58
Unferth and Breca, 30, 33, 48, 53–54, 61–63, 67
  sources of, 63
"Unferth Intermezzo," 62

V

vocabulary distribution of
  correlation with sources, 2
vocabulary, heterogeneity of, 38

W

warriors
  in the mead hall, 57
Wealhtheow, 27, 31, 60 (see also "Joy in the Hall"
Widsith, 77
Wiglaf, 27, 60
  entry into the barrow, 39
  upbraids cowardly retainers, 40
Wrenn, C. L.
  edition of *Beowulf*, 20
Wright, Charles J., 77
Wulfgar
  challenge of, 30

Z

Zupitza, Julius, 21

Printed by Printforce, the Netherlands